TRAPPING THE BOUNDARY WATERS

TRAPPING THE BOUNDARY WATERS

A TENDERFOOT IN THE BORDER COUNTRY, 1919-1920

CHARLES IRA COOK JR.
With an introduction by Harry B. Cook

MINNESOTA HISTORICAL SOCIETY PRESS

Foreword and text © 2000 by the Minnesota Historical Society. All rights reserved. No part of this book may be used or reproduced in any manner whatsoever without written permission except in the case of brief quotations embodied in critical articles and reviews. For information, write to the Minnesota Historical Society Press, 345 Kellogg Blvd. W., St. Paul, MN 55102-1906.

www.mhspress.org

The Minnesota Historical Society Press is a member of the Association of American University Presses.

Manufactured in the United States of America

10 9 8 7 6 5 4 3

♾ The paper used in this publication meets the minimum requirements of the American National Standard for Information Sciences—Permanence for Printed Library materials, ANSI Z39.48-1984.

All photographs are from the Harry B. Cook collection, Morton Grove, Illinois.

International Standard Book Number
ISBN 13: 978-0-87351-379-1 (paper)
ISBN 10: 0-87351-379-7 (paper)

Library of Congress
Cataloging-in-Publication Data

Cook, Charles Ira, 1892–1965.
  Trapping the boundary waters : a tenderfoot in the border country, 1919–1920 / Charles Ira Cook Jr.; with an introduction by Harry B. Cook.
     p. cm.
  ISBN 0-87351-379-7
     (pbk. : alk. paper)
  1. Cook, Charles Ira, 1892–1965.
  2. Pioneers—Minnesota—Boundary
     Waters Canoe Area Biography.
  3. Trappers—Minnesota—Boundary
     Waters Canoe Area Biography.
  4. Boundary Waters Canoe Area
     (Minn.) Biography.
  5. Boundary Waters Canoe Area
     (Minn.)—Description and travel.
  6. Outdoor life—Minnesota—
     Boundary Waters Canoe Area.
  I. Title II. Series
  FG12.B73.C66   2000
  977.6'7052'092—dc21
  [B]   99-40555
                                        CIP

TRAPPING THE BOUNDARY WATERS

Charles Ira Cook, Jr.

FOREWORD

"On May 4, 1919, looking like two disreputable junk peddlers at the end of a successful day, we started off. Our springs were flat, our purses flatter; the load pounded along on the rear axle, each bump in the road beating a tattoo on the seat of our pants that set our teeth to rattling. We were headed north for the Canadian border.... All summer lay before us in which to locate a jumping-off place from which we could say good-bye to civilization and head for the interior to establish our headquarters for the coming winter."

ON THIS OPTIMISTIC NOTE, my father, Charles Ira Cook Jr., began his youthful thirteen-month adventure in the Minnesota-Ontario Boundary Waters. Undeterred by his homesick companion's early departure, he set about learning to survive in the harsh northern wilderness.

He mastered canoeing, fishing, and sailing on windy lakes, cooking over an open fire, hunting game and fowl for food, and trapping for furs, the cash crop of the North. "Adopted" by trapper Bill Berglund, he came to know the Boundary Waters community of Indian and mixed-blood families and loners—guides, bootleggers, rangers, traders, and adventurers. He traveled by dogsled far into frozen Canada, where he finally reached the outer limits of his physical endurance—and lived to tell the tale to his family.

My father was born on November 30, 1892, in Menominee, Michigan, gateway to the Upper Peninsula. His father had managed a 6,400-acre family farm at Odebolt, Iowa, until it no longer paid well; he married my grandmother, Elizabeth Marie Paterson, in Chicago and moved to Menominee to go into business. Dad was the second of their three children.

Father spent a school year at Northwestern Military Academy in Lake Geneva, Wisconsin, three years at Lake Forest Academy in Illinois, and two years at the University of Wisconsin before his father called him home due to his lack of progress. He seems to have majored in fraternity life, fast cars (a Stutz Bearcat), and college girls. In 1917 he enlisted in what became the U.S. Army Air Service, training at Chanute Field in Rantoul, Illinois, rising to first lieutenant, earning his wings, and instructing pursuit pilots flying Jennys and de Havillands. While stationed at Lake Charles, Louisiana, he spent his free time apprenticed to a market duck hunter on the Gulf of Mexico. He also was stationed at Ellington Field in Houston, Texas, where he pioneered an airmail route.

Returning from the service in January 1919, my father worked—when he wasn't hunting or fishing—in most of his father's many businesses: wholesale groceries, dairy and produce farms, a spice factory, candy factory, cannery, pickle factory, and timber and iron mining interests in the Upper Peninsula.

Sometime in that next year, Charles Sr., who was unhappy with his son's frequent absences, said, "Charlie, get the hell out of here. Go north, and get the hunting and fishing out of your system because you are no damn good to me here!"

With sudden enthusiasm, my father and his friend Corney (Cornelius) Below loaded a Model-T Ford with camping essentials and headed for the northeastern Minnesota village of Winton, the jumping-off place for the recently established Superior National Forest. He added to his camping outfit at the store there and thence began the adventure recounted in this story.

In 1949 my father retired from a restless career as the owner of a logging operation at Rockland, Michigan, owner of the Cooks Pantry chain of twenty-two grocery stores, manager for the Kroger and Red Owl grocery chains, co-founder of Midland Cooperative Wholesale's grocery department and the Wissota grocery brokerage, district manager for the Office of Price Administration during World War II, and owner of Cooks Ice Cream, a dairy bar in Eau Claire, Wisconsin— in partnership with me after my discharge from the Army Signal Corps.

Dad's wilderness experiences, like other young people's risky undertakings, remained the high point of his life. I know, because I grew up on those stories, told and retold. I remember being sent off to bed only to sneak back to the head of the stairs to listen to him and my uncle, George Warner, yarning about those days.

Fondly remembering his youthful adventure, my father enrolled in writing courses and in the early 1950s typed up an account from memory of his "Wilderlust" excursion, as he called it. He wrote using some offensive but then common terms (deleted in this edition), and he approached Indian lifeways with the common stereotypes of his time. Many people will raise their eyebrows at some of his stories and call them tall tales, but my father said they were true. Maybe they are; maybe they aren't.

Knowing that he may not have correctly identified every lake he crossed nor every person he met, my father polished the manuscript as best he could. He then tried unsuccessfully to have it published. He died on February 6, 1965, at age seventy-two, content with his love of the outdoors and his contributions to his world.

I saved my father's penciled and typed manuscripts for four decades, keeping them in a box with his Air Corps wings and memorabilia from the adventure—rumpled maps and several dozen snapshots. Last year I came across a *Chicago Tribune* article by outdoors writer John Husar about Dorothy Molter, the Boundary Waters' Root Beer Lady. Molter was the life partner in later years of Bill Berglund, my father's first trapping partner. I called Mr. Husar, and he encouraged me to find a publisher for my father's story. Now, with the enthusiastic support of the Minnesota Historical Society Press, managing editor Ann Regan, and editors Marilyn Ziebarth and Deborah Swanson, I have done so.

My father came out of the north country in June of 1920 because of family pressure and, I think, a desire to get on with his life. He loaded two canoes with his take of furs, brought them down the "back way" to avoid American customs, and, packed in steamer trunks, they went by rail to a Chicago fur buyer. He concluded that his net profit of twelve hundred dollars was "not bad for those days." After reading his tale, I think you will agree.

HARRY B. COOK, DVM
June 1999

TRAPPING THE BOUNDARY WATERS

TECHNICALLY, WE WERE CITY PEOPLE; that is, my folks were born in Chicago. When a railroad company set out to grade, cut, and fill a roadbed westward across the Iowa plains, Grandfather, with advance knowledge of the route, had invested in a large tract of level prairie sod along the proposed right-of-way. Lush, wild buffalo grass, gray and dead-looking even in the flush of spring, hid beneath its somber coloring a food content that would support more cattle to the acre than any of the tame grasses then known to the agriculturists. It spread out over the entire farm, as far as the eye could see, broken only by the willow-bordered wrigglings of a creek that snaked diagonally across the five-mile length of the purchase, exposing the richness of the underlying dirt in the black softness of its crumbling banks. The farm lay to the south of the right-of-way and extended back for two miles, making a solid oblong of abundant pasture.

Father pioneered the area, and grew up a specialist in the raising of popcorn and white-faced cattle. This was back in the days when spring found the quail whistling their "bob-white" from every fence corner, and the prairie chickens answered from the stubble with their deep-throated "whoom-whoom." Yellowlegs, Father called them. As a boy, he roamed the prairie in an old buckboard behind a docile, rat-tailed chestnut mare called Jenny. Bones, a gaunt liver and white pointer with a stub tail, occupied the seat beside him. It was Jenny who really found the coveys, for from long experience she knew the kind of cover where the birds were most likely to be feeding. At this point Bones would take over, ranging the swales for a fresh scent. When he found one, he came to a stately point, made sure his quarry was not unduly alarmed at his presence, and looked back inquiringly over his shoulder to be sure Father had seen him. Then he would back quietly away and on cat's paws circle the near edges until the covey was bunched into a tight little group. By this time Father would have descended from the buckboard and come up to flush the birds. Bones did the retrieving and then set off ahead to point up the singles, most of which he had already marked down. The contempt with which he surveyed a miss was a reproof that only the most hardened could withstand without hanging their heads in shame, and on windy days when misses were frequent, Bones was apt to give up in disgust and head for home, as much as to say, "If you're not going to kill them, why should I bother to work my legs off hunting them up?" and no amount of persuasion could get him to return to the hunt.

Mother wouldn't consider living on the prairie, and Father had dreams of striking out for himself in a business of his own. That's how I happened to be born a swamp rabbit instead of a prairie clodhopper. At least, that's the way that Dad always told it.

Father came to the timber country to open up a banking business, but ended up as a wholesale grocer, supplying the big logging camps with mess pork, navy beans, and wheat flour for the men; hay and oats for the horses; and kerosene with which to illuminate the buildings for all. The business prospered, and I grew up in comparative ease and luxury, guided by an indulgent father and an imaginative mother, in a small frontier town on the northern peninsula of Michigan. The nightly ritual, "Once upon a time when Daddy was a little boy," beginning the hunting and fishing tales that lulled me to sleep in my father's lap, precluded any possibility that, in later years, my interests would lean in any other direction.

The press of business kept my father chained to an office chair most of the time, but in spite of his commercial activity he sandwiched in short periods of recreation that mollified his love of and longing for the open fields, the rushing streams, the marshy lakes, and the timbered wilderness. From the time I was fourteen years old, I was included in these excursions.

Our duck-hunting companion, Alec LaComb, was a French Canadian. He found for us the lakes that were most thickly populated with wild fowl, and while sleepy stars, their night of vigil almost over, blinked drowsily in the gray shivering dawn, he could sniff the awakening flutter of a breeze and pick with unerring accuracy the points of rush where the morning flights would be most heavily concentrated. From him I learned the habits of these feathered creatures, their food, their haunts, and their colorings. As far as the eye could see, I could distinguish between the long, thick neck and slow wing of the mallard; the short, stubby neck and plump body of the canvasback with his shorter wing; the boring down flight and fast flicker of the short wing of a teal; and the long, stretched-out silhouette of the pintail with the scythe-shaped pinion. He taught me to imitate their calls without the aid of mechanical devices, to distinguish between the sharp notes of alarm, the voice of challenge, the call of a mate, and the soft, satisfied feeding chuckles of a hungry flock. I learned their style of flight in formation, the manner in which they descended from high altitudes, and their method of takeoff from the water. It was the thrill of a lifetime to turn, with soft vocal persuasions, the wary green-headed leader of a flock of mallards so that the entire flight would swing in confidently over our decoys, set their wings, and put on the brakes preparatory to making a landing.

Fred Stephanson, the leader of our deer-hunting crowd, was an internationally known sportsman who followed the seasons around the world. He had been in Africa with the late Carl Akeley, a taxidermist and explorer formerly of the Field Museum of Natural History in Chicago and later curator of the American Museum of Natural History in New York City. The fine group specimens of African wildlife now on display in the Field Museum are the trophies of that trip. He had hunted geese in Louisiana; ducks in Virginia; quail in Mississippi; prairie chickens in Dakota; pheasants in the central and western states; mountain lion in Texas and Mexico; antelope, elk, and bear in the Midwest; moose in Canada; and Kodiaks in Alaska. He had gunned with royalty in Russia, England, and Germany, on the private preserves of great country estates.

Our party opened the ruffed grouse season in Michigan, shooting over the most magnificent specimens of Llewellyn (English) setters you have ever seen, field trial champions from Fred's numerous kennels. We hunted deer a hundred miles to the north in an uninhabited sanctuary, where one hundred and fifty thousand acres of virgin timber, owned by the lumber barons, gave us an unequaled preserve that was overrun with whitetails.

Here again I was under the tutelage of a master, a hunter born with the instinct of the wild. Our party, with the exception of Fred, were older men like Father, escaping momentarily from the cares of business life. This gave Fred time to take me under his wing, and I acted as his lieutenant while he organized our drives and planned our strategy. For the first week of our stay we worked ceaselessly to assist the older men of the party in obtaining the quota without taxing their latent muscles. We placed them on runways and worked the pockets, swamps, and nearby thickets, literally dropping opportunities for a shot into their laps, so that they could return home and display the fruits of their prowess and recount the stories of their kills to the patient wives and suffering friends at home. During the last three days, Fred and I struck farther afield and were usually fortunate enough to not only fill our own licenses, but also complete the unfilled remainder for the camp.

Many old-timers will scoff at this, but Fred could smell 'em! During the rutting season, I have frequently been conscious of a strong goaty odor when dressing out a buck. This is particularly true of the old ones, but I cannot lay claim to having noticed the scent while the animal was still on the hoof. Time and again, however, still hunting upwind through the timber with Fred, I had seen him suddenly stop and sample the air. There would be a nervous snort from a thicket up ahead, and the sound of running hoofs, or we would glimpse a vanishing white flag taking off through the trees.

On one occasion our entire party had just left camp

following a well-defined trail that led up through the timber. A crosswind blew in off two open popple [aspen] ridges that paralleled the trail some forty yards to our right. As we came abreast of the opening, Fred halted the party, turned off the trail, and cautiously approached the ridges, signaling me to follow. We climbed the first one and, reaching the top, I drew up alongside. Twenty feet below us a two-hundred-and-fifty-pound buck had bedded down on the hillside. The ridge had prevented his hearing our approach and he lay facing away from us, nose into the wind. What devilish impulse prompted Fred's actions I do not know, but he suddenly made a terrific leap, landing with a terrifying whoop on the rump of the reclining animal. The buck lurched to his feet and struck with his horns, putting a sharp prong completely through the meaty part of Fred's calf. The deer then charged off, cutting back through a break in the ridge to our rear, where I put a bullet through his heart. Fred's hunting was over for that season, for aside from the fact that the wound was very painful, it became infected from shreds of wool sock that had been driven into the hole by the force of the blow. His keen sense of smell in this case had been his undoing.

For an impressionable youngster, this background ensured a keen interest in the outdoor life. Around the glowing sides of our potbellied camp stoves we gathered in the evening, and I listened with awe to the tales of far-off lands and the wilderness adventures of my more traveled associates.

My own side trips to these annual deluxe events, with boys of my own age, were purely thermos-bottle excursions. Our mothers packed our lunches, we drove the family car to our destinations, and, after hunting or fishing for the day, or at most the weekend, we were back in our own warm beds without a care in the world.

Fired by my own experiences and the tales of my elders, the seed of adventure had been sown on fertile soil. I dreamed of continuing where I had left off, of going beyond the outposts of civilization and exploring the far-off places, where man had seldom ventured. What an experience it would be to rough it through all the seasons. This idea never left me.

About this time a new expedition to Africa was being contemplated, and to my great delight I was included in the plans. Two years on this darkest continent! What an experience to look forward to! Preparations, planning, outfitting, correspondence—everything was almost complete, and then came the war. My most cherished plans collapsed overnight.

The war, however, presented a new diversion, and almost immediately I enlisted, passed my physical examinations, and launched myself upon a new experience, the exploration of the air, for I had enrolled in the Army Air Service. Nearly three years of this new existence, then came the Armistice. Just in time, too, for flying to me had become no more exciting than driving the family flivver down Main Street. This was the end. I came back home footloose, restless, and unhappy. I had seen everything and done everything; what further thrill could life hold?

I voiced this unrest to Cornelius Below, my boyhood companion, and expressed the desire to spend a year in the wilderness before settling down to the inevitable desk in my father's office. "Corney," as we called him, jumped at the suggestion, and we solemnly shook hands on a pact which bound us to a full year's trip of exploration and adventure. What preparations we made! We studied maps of the northern continent, picked out the uninhabited sections to which rivers and lake chains offered the only means of access, and numbered them for investigation in their order. We purchased a secondhand car of fairly late vintage which the mechanic assured us had, at worst, only a slight arterial murmur that would not interfere with its faithful performance for some time to come. We stowed eighteen hundred pounds of equipment, guns, ammunition, fishing tackle, winter and summer clothing, bedding, food, traps, and more into its bathtub body, and our preparations were complete.

On May 4, 1919, looking like two disreputable junk peddlers at the end of a successful day, we started off. Our springs were flat, our purses flatter; the load pounded along on the rear axle, each bump in the road beating a tattoo on the seat of our pants that set our teeth to rattling. We were headed north for the Canadian border. On the way up, we stopped for several days along our favorite trout streams as a last good-bye to the more genteel type of sportsman's life. There was plenty of time; all summer lay before us in which to locate a jumping-off place from which we could say good-bye to civilization and head for the interior to establish our headquarters for the coming winter.

PICTURE A SMALL LUMBERING TOWN deserted when the timber ran out, standing at the foot of a lake, buildings sinking into decay, forlorn, left behind by seekers of new forests to plunder. The houses stood in empty rows, their jaundiced hollow-eyed windows staring out of the dusk with their bloodshot reflections of the sinking sun, reminiscent of more prosperous days gone before. The barn-red paint scaled from their warping sides, and the window-high weeds in the yards gave them the look of dissolute lumberjacks with a week's growth of beard, sitting there waiting, waiting to hear again the song of the saw and the woods cry of "Timber!" This was Winton after the war, the northernmost town in the lake country of eastern Minnesota, and the terminus of the Duluth and Iron Range Railroad. From here on, the hardy traveler took to canoes in summer and dogsleds in winter to penetrate the vast expanse of wilderness that lay to the north. The land o' lakes, wildlife, and timber, the home of beauty and adventure for those who sought escape from the cares of civilization. Some thirty inhabitants still remained: the caretaker for the lumber company, the derelict, and the few hardy souls who were still hopeful of wresting an existence from the lakes and streams by guiding, trapping, and fishing. The lone storekeeper, who seemed to sit astride his stock in trade like a defiant dog guarding the bone from which all trace of meat had long since vanished, directed us to the caretaker who had charge of the company houses.

This grizzled old backwoodsman—who, it was at once

apparent, had found solace in the bottle during his long vigil over the ghost of the past that had been left in his charge — not only offered us a seven-room house, but, by the time he had finished our only quart of medicinal whiskey, which we had carefully guarded, gave us a garage as well, all for four dollars per month. This afforded us ample space in which to store our car and those of our effects which we wished to leave behind during our first trip of exploration into the interior. We were cautioned that we needed a guide, that the rivers were treacherous, and that only game trails connected the waterways. We were well fortified with maps, compasses, and ego, as well as a proud belief in our own ability as sourdoughs,* and therefore disdained his offer to find us capable assistants for our trip. Replenishing our food supply that night, we were gone before daylight the next morning, our folding canvas canoe precariously loaded, blissfully unconscious of the disasters that just one hidden snag or sharp rock could cause us a hundred miles back in the wilderness. The day dawned bright and cloudless; Fall Lake was as still and reflective as a pan of quicksilver and threw back images that vied for honors with the beautiful shoreline. In fact, a picture taken that morning of some white paper birch clinging to a rocky promontory defied us later to tell which was the subject and which the reflection.

The whole universe, as we surveyed it, was alive. Birds called from the shores, fish leaped or left concentric rings on the surface as they broke the water in feeding. Far down the lake a loon pierced the stillness with its chilly, vacant laugh.

---

* A complimentary term for men who lived in the bush. They often carried fermented batter for preparing breadstuffs.

Our pulses quickened to the excitement as the village passed out of sight behind a point and our paddles sent gurgling whorls spinning dizzily in the wake of our speeding canoe. We soon slowed our exuberant sprint, however, and settled down to a slower but mile-consuming pace as our muscles, unaccustomed to the strain, complained of their conscription.

On this, the first of the lakes we were to travel and less than eight miles out of town, we saw our first deer. He came tumbling out of the brush and spilled into the water just ahead of us as though startled by some unseen marauder in the darkness of the thicket. Striking out majestically, he crossed in front of our canoe in great surges, so close that we could see the little beads of water clinging to the velvet of his young horns like pearls on the plush mat of a jeweler's counter. We paddled on in hushed silence, each aware of the thrill the other had experienced in these evidences of the sportsman's paradise we were entering.

Noon found us well along the first leg of our journey. We began to run into numerous islands, sharp heaps of fractured granite whose sides broke the surface at right angles to the water. There was hardly a place to land and no vegetation except some scraggly cedars whose roots grasped the rocky surfaces like an eagle's talons and sent tiny tendrils from their undersides down into the crevices. In the hollows, we found a luxuriant growth of moss almost two feet thick. Through ages of struggle for life, these primitive plants had combed the dust particles from the air and stored them around their roots, the meager soil to which they owed their very existence.

Wet with perspiration, we lodged the point of our canoe

between two fragments of stone on the shore of one of these rock islands, removed our clothes, and took to the icy waters for a refreshing swim. From a precipitous overhang some twenty feet high, we dove down until our hearts beat a thunderous tattoo against our ribs, but we were unable to hold our breath long enough to reach the bottom of this deep lake bed. What terrific, relentless power, what angry disturbances there must have been to gouge out such scars in a field of solid granite, and how quickly Mother Nature had healed these unsightly woods with this beautiful expanse of water, truly a masterpiece of plastic surgery. In our hurry to leave the world behind us, we gulped a cold lunch which only partially satisfied our ravenous appetites, lay down on the soft moss for a rest and a short smoke, and then pushed on into the beyond.

It was a lazy afternoon and we dozed over the rhythmic slosh of our paddles in complete contentment. Round a point of sandy shore, our sleepy semiconsciousness was suddenly shattered, and we both galvanized into life with an excited, "Look!" At the same moment, we had both spotted a large mother black bear and her two new cubs feeding on a dead fish that had washed ashore. The mother rose slowly on her hind legs, looked us over carefully, and with a derisive snort lumbered off into the nearby bushes with her two cubs close at her heels. This was indeed a paradise. Fall Lake, then Newton; we could now look ahead and from our maps plot a course for the spot where we hoped to find the river that connected us with Pipestone Bay, the next body of water to cross. Our energies revived, and we presently nosed the canoe in a dead heat with its own reflection onto a sandy shore near the river's mouth. The map showed a distance of about three-fourths of a mile separating the two lakes, and a well-beaten path marked our course following the river across the portage. Our first indication that all was not paradise came as we disturbed the bushes that overhung the trail. Clouds of mosquitoes took wing to dive on our unprotected parts, and we were forced to lighten our loads in order to take an occasional whack at the more painful bites we were receiving. In addition to these marauders, countless blackflies settled on our necks and crawled up our sleeves, to lend their hot-lead-like sting to our discomfort. Three trips put us on the shore of the bay, and we pitched our tent and made ready for the night on a grassy slope a stone's throw from the water.

Halfway across the portage, the slatelike strata of the riverbed had faulted, forming Pipestone Falls, a beautiful sheer drop of thirty feet. The water rounded over the brink of the chasm in such endless unity that it seemed to almost stand still, as if poured of molten glass. Below, it boiled into the pool amidst sprays of rainbowed mist with a roar that defied conversation.

We had been told by our new landlord that this spot contained some fine walleyes, and we anticipated feasting that night on their sweet, nutlike meat. Hurrying back with our tackle for the first cast, we waded out waist deep into the turbulent waters and, reels singing, sent our lures into exciting eddies. Clunk! At almost every cast, there was a rush, our lines twanged like bowstrings, shaking feathers of mist from their lengths as we sunk home the hook. Now we gave ground, thumbing our reels, poles arching with the strain, as our quarries braved the rapids or headed for the bottom of a deep pool, there to sulk and contemplate their fate. We hauled out gleaming, golden beauty after beauty. Suddenly, my elation cooled. It is surprising the value man places on his accomplishments. We were having the thrill of a lifetime, but what would we do with the fish? There was no audience, no one to exclaim over the fruits of our prowess, and there were no victims to consume our surplus. Our catch became nothing more than food to us, and we had already taken more than enough for that purpose. Regretfully we returned to camp and cooked our evening meal, the first of many to be taken from the lakes and streams we were to travel. The pike were delicious, and we stuffed ourselves into a lethargy that would not be denied. The dishes washed, time out for a smoke, and we were soon fast asleep on our not too uncomfortable bed of spruce boughs.

One would have thought we were two old men as we prepared to leave in the morning, and it was fully an hour after pushing off from the shore before we had the kinks out of our stiff, cramped muscles. There were three more short, painful portages before we reached Basswood Lake, the first of the border chain, but here luck was with us. With dark, angry scowls, some fast-scudding clouds in the west puffed out their cheeks and blew down the four-and-a-half miles of water a stiff breeze that whipped up foot-high waves on its indigo surface. We decided to chance it, to rig up a sail and run before the wind to save a long, grueling paddle. A short, stocky popple did for the mast and a smaller one for a crossarm, to which we lashed an old blue army blanket. There was plenty of clothesline for guys, and we tied shorter pieces to each of the two lower corners of the blanket so that we could square our sail to catch the wind.

More experienced mariners would not have attempted the crossing, and in no time we were in trouble. As we left the lee of the shore and caught the full impact of the wind, we could feel the canoe strain forward, mounting the waves and balancing precariously on their crests, our prow and stern completely out of water. The weight of our load and the support of such a small surface of the lake admidship settled us low in the swells, and the crowns of the rollers caught up to us, spilling over the thwarts into our canoe as we rushed along. The stem split the surface with the sound of escaping steam, ending in a chuckling gurgle as each mountain of sea passed beneath us, dropping us back into the following trough. It was a race with the elements. One moment we surged ahead, picking up speed, and it would seem as though we must surely leave the surface and fly with the gales that leaned so insistently against our blanket, then, as if an unseen hand reached up and pulled us down again, we lagged behind, wallowing in the backwash.

What a thrilling ride it was! Our taut muscles twanged out vibrant, chorded chills that ran the scale up and down our spines, but the seriousness of our predicament was brought forcefully to our attention as the water rose steadily and slopped around our ankles in the bottom of the canoe. Corney sat in the stern handling the paddles, which we used for a rudder, and I held the ropes that guided our makeshift sail. So far, by manipulating these halyards and with the help of the paddle, we had been able to maintain a course straight on down the lake, but we were carrying too much canvas and I was forced to relinquish the guys. This cut our blanket down to an inverted triangle with the base above at the crossarm and the point where it met the mast, the released lower corners slapping noisily on each side. I was kneeling in three inches of water, and with the situation eased slightly I was now free to bail urgently with my hat. Breakers continued to pour over the sides and the depth of the water in the canoe gained steadily. We were slowly sinking and there was nothing to do but continue on our course toward the rocky shoreline, where we faced another formidable hazard. The crossarm that supported our sail had been securely lashed to the mast, and the footing was too precarious for us to attempt to stand up long enough to undo our folly. In the end, this bit of seeming stupidity may have been our salvation, for we were traveling along almost as fast as the waves themselves, which prevented their curling in over our stern as well as over the sides. Nearing the shore, the canoe half full of water, we saw a possible way to avoid disaster and jumped overboard, landing chest deep in the lake, guiding our canoe as rapidly as possible through the jagged rocks. We could not escape the sea but clung firmly to the gunwales as it came crashing down upon us. For the moment we were completely submerged, the force of the impact throwing us violently shoreward, but we regained our footing and struggled up the bank out of danger.

Fortunately, our food was packed in a double-tied waterproof duffel bag, and only a little moisture seeped in. Our flour, sugar, and cornmeal all were dry. A little tea was moistened, but we dried it out and could not taste the difference.

The tent, blankets, and clothing were another matter. They were in ordinary packsacks and were soaked to the core. After inspecting the damage and sorting out our possessions, we built a roaring fire, set up our tent downwind and tied up the side walls so that the heat could penetrate, wrung out our blankets and clothes and spread them on the bushes to dry. We wiped off and oiled our guns and other gear, turning and shifting our blankets between times, so that when night fell we slept quite comfortably by draping our forms around the few damp spots still left in our bedding.

Breakfast over, we packed hurriedly, loaded and balanced our canoe, and again took to the lake. Paddling and portaging were no longer torture, for our muscles were firming rapidly, tuning themselves to these new exertions. I no longer noticed in my bed the bough ribs which I had failed to cover sufficiently with the softer, finer needles of the spruce, and at night I slept as one drugged until the warmth of the morning sun stirred my blood and I awakened to the toil and joy of another day.

Our maps showed this, the seventh lake we had crossed, to be the jumping-off place, for the portages from here on were mere dots and not well-defined trails as shown on the vacationers' routes. Prairie Portage was the last of the tenderfoot trails. Beyond was the wilderness, the unknown, where deer and moose, otter and beaver, wolf and lynx, as well as the many smaller furbearers, battled for their right to existence, disturbed only in winter when the hardy Indian and white trappers sought them for their pelts. Here too we would try our skill when the snow came, but there were still miles to travel and lots to do. We must push on, farther from the scars of civilization, closer to the apex of this raw, timbered kingdom, before picking the site for our new cabin home.

We crossed this small lake in a matter of minutes and were surprised to note that it was dark and muddy and much warmer than the clear, cold water of Basswood, the big lake we had sailed the day before. Again, Birch Lake, the next in the chain, was clear, spring-fed water. From here, we entered a long, very narrow lake through a navigable stream much to our liking, for no portages were necessary. Knife Lake also was quite dark and the water the color of thin tea, but again it was much colder. The Indians had told us we could find some fine landlocked salmon here, but by this time we had reached the end of our patience and thought only of arriving at our destination. We did not even take time out for so civilized an act as rod fishing; instead we trailed a copper lure with a single hook behind the canoe on a hundred yards of line tied to the thwart. It was necessary to troll to the end of the lake and halfway back again before we had a strike, but our efforts were rewarded and we hauled in a red and blue speckled beauty whose colors shaded the rainbow. I have no doubt that the darker waters accentuated his coloring, for I had never before seen one that did not have a faded appearance, while this one looked freshly done in bright oils. There was still time for one more lake, and we were anxious to find better water for drinking purposes and a possible cold plunge after setting up camp.

The inlet to the next lake was likewise a navigable stream, and we pushed slowly up against the current. Around the first bend, a large female black bear, rump toward us, stood in the middle of the stream on some flat rocks below a riffle. She was as motionless as the rocks themselves, her head lowered, gazing intently into a small pool which formed at the base of the rapids. She had shifted her eight or nine hundred pounds of weight* so that one forepaw was poised ready for a lightning thrust into the dark depths, should an unwary succulent trout rest for a moment before attempting the swift water ahead. The splashing and gurgling of the tumbling stream drowned the sound of our approach, and we hesitated to come closer to this mountain of destruction for fear a cub lay on the bank waiting for his supper. In that case she might have turned on us, and we were much in favor of the cub's dining on fish; however, she suddenly wheeled, leaped ashore, and disappeared into the bushes. I could have touched her with my paddle. She must have seen our shadow in the pool, or been guided by that instinct of the wild that warns of danger, for I am sure she did not hear us. Possibly at that close range she had smelled us, even though we were downwind from her. It was nothing short of miraculous to see the speed and agility with which this huge, clumsy-looking animal vanished into the surrounding cover.

There was insufficient water in the rapids to float our canoe, and the canvas bottom crunched ominously over the shoals as we waded upstream, but finally we reached deeper water and paddled out onto the spring-fed expanse of Cypress Lake.

Up until now, the wooded areas had been covered with alder brush, popple thickets, young birch, maple and ash

* An eight- or nine-hundred-pound female bear is probably a hunter's exaggeration.

saplings; occasionally, a derelict pine that had escaped the lumberman's saw because of some imperfection stood lonesomely above the second growth, a silent sentinel of the past. In contrast, this glistening body of water was completely surrounded by towering Norway and white pine, standing at attention like tall, copper-skinned warriors. Eighty feet in the air, they broke out into green-plumed helmets which camouflaged their naked brown bodies as if from an expected aerial enemy.

We pitched camp in this forest of giants and barely found room to place our tent among them. No stakes or poles were necessary. We merely tied our guy lines to the trunks of the trees that crowded us, and ran a rope between two trees for our ridgepole. Our beds were ready-made for us by the inches of soft brown needles that covered the ground.

Have you ever eaten fresh-caught landlocked salmon, drenched in butter, the delicate pink meat cooked and golden-crusted over an open fire? Add to that potatoes baked in the coals, fresh hot biscuits, wild raspberries, and the pipes of Pan playing an accompanying symphony in the pine tops, and you have a banquet setting to delight the wanderer who feels and appreciates the magnificence of nature's handicraft. We lazed away the twilight in well-fed contentment, satisfied to be gazing across the placid waters and into the verdant depths of the forest beyond until night folded its blue shadows over us and the hushed beauty of our surroundings. The coals of our campfire blinked drowsily and a thin wisp of smoke curled lazily upward to fan out into a scenic railway of hooks and turns, dips and inclines, drifting and threading its wraithlike way among the trees. Fantasies such as these, and the sweet scent of the pines, carried us off into the misty future of our dreams before we could arouse sufficiently to pull up our blankets.

"Come and get it!" The phantom perfumes of the night before were displaced by the reality of cooking odors, steaming coffee, hotcakes, and bacon. I had overslept, and breakfast was served! A dash of cold lake water in my face and over the upper half of my torso chased the sleep from my eyes and speeded the blood through my veins. A vigorous rubdown, and I fell to hungrily in just my shorts. The sun had not penetrated sufficiently for insects to start their depredations, and the chill of the morning dew started little shivers chasing each other among the goose pimples on my body. After breakfast, a shirt, khaki breeches, and moccasins, and I was dressed for the day.

At an earlier date, someone had cut an avenue through the pines that marked the next portage. Rangers possibly, or government surveyors clearing a way through which they could sight their transits. We found evidences of this as we crossed. A lone solid bronze obelisk, painted a questionable white and anchored in concrete, stood beside the trail. It must have weighed at least two hundred pounds. On the south side, we read the words "United States" and on the north, "Canada." Seventy-five miles from a settlement, and still we could not get away from the signs that man had been there before us. We later learned that the borders, even in these far-off reaches, had been distinctly defined by permanent markers separating the two countries. Large crews with a dozen or more canoes had braved the hardships of the unknown to pack their way through miles upon miles of timber and swampland that for many years to come would not again be invaded by anyone other than Indians and trappers.

Our next lake was a large one dotted with thousands of small islands. One group resembled a mighty battleship and her consorts. The largest one, camouflaged in dark shaded patches of evergreen spaced by lighter shades of birch, maple, and aspen, carried two massive funnels, the trunks of age-old pine shattered just above the level of the surrounding growth during an electrical storm in years gone by. Her spars: naked bodies of dried spruce, slanting slightly aft, were complete even to spike-limbed yardarms. In one of these an eagle's aerie perched high in the rigging to simulate a crow's nest, and along her sides bright beams of sunlight filtered through small breaks in foliage like the lights from blinking portholes. Clustered around the formidable battle wagon, and strung out in perfect formation heading into the wind, were countless other ships of lesser degree, flat-tops, destroyers, and tenders to the mother ship, all riding calmly at anchor under her protection. This was Big Saganaga, one of the largest lakes of the border chain.

The sky over the first island we came to was alive with graceful white herring gulls. This was their mating season. They wheeled and turned on motionless wings, soaring and diving, keeping up an incessant, raucous clamor which increased in intensity as we drew near. The island itself was white with nesting birds that took wing as we landed, adding to the commotion by screaming their protest at our invasion of their sanctuary. We found hundreds of nests, mere depressions in the rocky ground, lined with bits of well-rotted wood and an occasional feather or two, in which lay one to three olive-tan eggs generously sprinkled with black. They were the size of a small pullet egg. We slit two curved pieces of bark from the bole of a large birch and cut oval openings, slightly smaller than the eggs, in their centers. By holding these makeshift candlers closely in front of our faces, like a Halloween mask to shut out the light, it was possible to face the sun, cover the oval opening with an egg, and determine with reasonable accuracy the fertility of our harvest. Taking only a small percentage of their efforts, we knew that these would be replaced by fresh layings soon after the birds discovered their loss. We dined on sea gull eggs for several days, carrying our surplus carefully packed in rotted wood.

As we progressed across the lake, we steered by compass, round island after island and taking up our course again by approximation on the other side. Time after time we thought we had reached shore and hunted for our portage, when suddenly we would round a point and enter another island-dotted bay. Ultimately we saw ahead a low-lying bog edged with drooping alders and covered with a dense growth of cranberry bushes. Dead spikes of spruce dotted this morass, and here and there a young green sapling bravely struggled to survive the inevitable death by drowning suffered by its predecessors during the spring floods. It did not immediately occur to us that we were lost, for surely we were in the vicinity of the portage for which we had so carefully plotted our course. Round the last little spruce-tufted island snuggling against this background of dismal swamp, we were distracted for the moment from the seriousness of our predicament.

There in the narrow channel, herding her brood of

eleven tiny balls of blue-black velvet down, sat a large mother loon.* She was as surprised as we were, but at a low guttural command the little fellows all dove and scattered. The mother, fluttering pitifully, lying on her side and kicking in circles as though mortally wounded, did all in her power to center our attention on her while she continued to warn her young and urge them to cover in the tall grasses and overhanging bushes. The little fellows could not have been more than a day or so out of the egg, and their little lungs did not have the capacity for submerging any great length of time. Paddling swiftly, we cut them off from the shore and concentrated on capturing one of the brood. By staying close, we kept him underwater so constantly that he was completely exhausted in a matter of minutes and we were able to pick him up and place him on top of a packsack in the prow of our canoe to sit for his picture. Just as we lifted our little captive from the water he uttered a pitiful little cry for help, and his little black eyes glanced with fear in all directions for some means of escape from these strange surroundings; but for the time being he rested, awaiting the opportune moment for a try at freedom.

Loons, like all diving birds, are poor fliers. They must have a long expanse of water from which to rise and gain altitude, for their progress, like a heavily laden plane's, is slow and they obtain flying speed only with great effort. Their small, narrow, tapered wings, with their short, heavily ribbed pinions, are much better adapted to powerful thrusts underwater. In this heavier medium, they can propel themselves with great speed and agility, and are able to provide for

* Loons normally hatch one or two chicks.

themselves and their young from the many species of fish on which they feed.

In her hour of need, this courageous mother rose laboriously from the water in a miraculous short distance to render assistance to her offspring, and with loud, shrill cries, banked sharply and came at us time after time with a display of courage that only mother love could muster. Closer and closer she came with each onslaught and finally, in one last desperate charge, her supreme moment of sacrifice, she dove straight at us, her lancelike beak poised for the fatal thrust— a Don Quixote charging the windmill. There was a sound of ripping canvas as her knife-sharp beak cut a six-inch gash in the bow of the canoe, and our attacker fell back into the lake, stunned from the shock of the blow she had dealt. Diving beneath the surface instantly, she came up some distance away and shepherded the stragglers of her little flock to safety. Apparently she had given up the unfortunate one who sat disconsolately astride our pack. For a time, the mother absorbed our attention, but we finally got a photograph and dropped our little captive over the side, where he paddled desperately for shore, uttering short, inquiring peeps as he went. We did not see the mother again nor hear any answering instructions, but he reached the safety of the marsh and disappeared from view.

This exciting interlude temporarily took our minds off our own predicament, but the question now arose as to which way we should travel to find our portage. There was no sign of an opening in either direction, nor any cleft in the trees on the skyline that might indicate a trail; it was a matter of conjecture as to where we explored first. The closest big timber lay to the north and we headed in that direction, watching the shoreline carefully for any sign of a little used, overgrown trail that might be our destination. There was little need to paddle our entire outfit on our search for the portage, so we pitched our tent beneath a canopy of tall pines and decided not to break camp again until we had found it.

Some shoemaker's thread and marine glue from the emergency kit repaired the rent in the prow to our satisfaction, and we set about putting everything in shape for a quick takeoff in the morning. Odds and ends that we had carelessly thrown in the canoe on previous stops were repacked into a minimum number of pieces for quick handling. We swam and washed clothes in the lake and, aside from ironing, were as spic and span as debutantes at a coming-out ball, a rather unlikely occurrence in that immediate neighborhood.

Traveling light the next day, we continued northward with enough food for three meals, a fish line, and a small-caliber pistol as our only luggage. We made excellent time, as our canoe hardly drew any water at all, and explored minutely each bay and creek we came to. We walked for miles on deer trails and up skidways along which the beaver had hauled their popple cuttings to the lake for winter storage. Each time our hopes faded at seeing the trails diverging and losing themselves in timber or thicket as each member of the wild went his individual way. Slowly the shoreline turned westward until we knew there was no longer any hope of finding our opening in this direction, as the portage was definitely on the east shore of the lake. The next day we paddled far to the south, going through the same procedure as before, and gave up only when our course became predominantly west. It took a great deal of reckoning and many extra miles of travel to determine beyond all question our general direction; many times we almost met ourselves coming back as we rounded a hook of land, completely reversing our direction only to find that we were directly opposite from where we had been earlier in the day, across a narrow peninsula of land. In one instance, we did portage out of one of these bays back into the main lake across a strip of land less than twenty feet wide and saved ourselves miles of fruitless backtracking. It took us two more days of careful searching without results before we were ready to give up and retrace our steps to make a new start, reckoning from the point where we had entered the lake.

As a rule, woodsmen and explorers leave some sign by which they can retrace their routes or by which those who follow can more easily find the hidden passages. A lopped off tree or two, a blaze on the trunk of a larger tree, or an old rag tied onto a carefully trimmed top of a supple sapling that springs high above the surrounding growth when released will mark the more-traveled trails.

On the fifth day, we packed up and headed back to where we had disturbed the peace and happiness of the little family of loons and took our compass reading for the return trip across the lake. There was no sign of life and I scoured the shore where the little downy wild things had so quickly blended with the shadows in their flight. You had heard the simile "as crazy as a loon." This gibberish stems from the loon's long, lonesome, high-pitched call, ending on a moaning note, that so often breaks the silence of the wilderness in the middle of the night, like the wailing of a lost and forgotten soul echoing in some stark asylum dungeon for the mentally deranged. I stared vacantly at this shoreline, deep in recollection, until slowly it crept upon me that I was looking straight at the mouth of quite a sizable creek. True, it was grown over with alders, but had we not been distracted we would most certainly have found it on the first try. If anyone was crazy, we were. We had hit the portage on the very first trip, but this inanimate object had been backgrounded by the more interesting discovery of the family of loons, and we had gone past without noticing the opening. At any rate, we were ready to go and, parting the brush, we wedged up the stream, pushing our way by the hummocks of marsh grass along the bank. It was disgusting to think that we had wasted four whole days by our stupidity.

Halfway up the marsh the creek veered in toward high land, and an easily distinguishable trail led up over the hill. As we packed across this dividing ridge, we looked down a cool green vista of foliage and out across pale blue waters in an inscrutable forest of pine, spruce, and cedar in deep Robin Hood greens, shadowed by a sheer cliff of variegated granite that served as a backdrop to the silent depths. From the heights, slender popple and white birch in their pastel colors waved dreamily at the points of receding, saw-toothed conifers that reached out into the lake to enfold the cool, inviting bays. Following the shoreline, we picked up some walleyes for supper and searched the bays for a sheltered spot to camp.

On the far side of the second head of land, a large moose

cow stood shoulder deep in the lake among some lily pads, her head completely underwater. We froze into statues immediately. Finally she came up for air, her mouth dripping succulent lily roots which she slowly devoured as she scanned the countryside for possible danger. Satisfied, she again submerged, and we sprang into action. Paddling fiercely in her direction and keeping in the shadow of the shore, freezing each time she surfaced, we were almost upon her as we drove our canoe forward for the last sprint. Taken completely by surprise, she turned and lunged for the bank, pushing a wall of water and spray in front of her, and disappeared into the forest in long, stiff-legged strides.

At the end of the bay and beyond a pebbly beach lay a beautiful well-kept greensward, the grass cropped close and sloping gently up from the water like a landscaped summer resort lawn. For the moment, we expected to see a mansion peeping at us from the trees, but found this cool inviting spot to be nothing more than nature's superb artistry, the lawn and hedges well tended by her herbivorous caretakers. We had come some ninety miles by canoe in our travels and that night, between flipping fish in our frying pan and poking the boiling potatoes suspended over the fire, we studied our maps and resolved to spend the morrow in exploration.

We were well beyond the rim of human activity; the timber was dense and the game trails numerous. There had been a great many beaver and muskrat houses along the route, and we had encountered deer, bear, and moose, and frequently exclaimed at the number and variety of ducks that used these lakes for their flyways. Wood ducks, mergansers, and mallards predominated, but there were also little flocks of teal, butterball, and black duck that hurried by. The rice bays were full of coots nesting and waiting for the succulent wild rice to head out and pass the milk stage, when they would dine sumptuously and fatten for the strenuous southern migration. Grebe dove for snails and mud minnows among the water plants, and marsh wrens and red-winged blackbirds sang joyously from swaying grass perches along the shore. From early morning on, far into the night, partridge beat their wings against their favorite drum logs,* producing a rhythmic concussion that sounded like the dull booming of a far-distant motorboat engine, the tempo increasing until the reports came so close together that they blended into the rattle of a snare drum. Little birds twittered, warbled, chirped, and cooed, making love in the trees and bushes, while chicken hawks, ospreys, and black eagles wheeled and turned in motionless circles high overhead. This was spring in a wildlife sanctuary.

To the north, our Canadian map showed a lake which we estimated at about two miles long by one-half mile wide, some four miles distant over land. There were no water connections with the chain we had been following and no trails we could find to enter on; this was just as we wanted it. What would it hold in store for the explorer? Our compass course took us across rough, rolling, high country. There were mixed hardwoods and conifers, but the growth was as heavy as we had camped in for the past three nights, and the going was easy. We paused frequently to take a sight with our compass on some new landmark ahead that would keep

* Partridge, a local term for the ruffed grouse, beat their wings together over their backs.

us on a straight course. Any error in our reckoning and we could easily miss the lake and walk on and on before realizing our mistake. We had dubbed our destination Lake Expectancy. The sun was warm, and enough filtered through the foliage so that our exertions caused our bodies to steam freely, little rivulets of perspiration running down our backs. Eventually, we glimpsed the waters of our lake through the trees and knew our calculations had been perfect. From a narrow white birch point we could look up and down the shore for about a mile in either direction.

Two days' supply of food, a gun, our canoe, two squares of canvas, and some mosquito netting were all we packed in with us, and with the canvas and netting we improvised a pup tent (of a sort) that would shelter us for the night. Of course, we had the inevitable ax, tea pail, and frying pan as well as our sheath knives, all of which had, by now, become as much a part of us as our hands and feet, and equally as useful. There were a great many waterfowl on this lake, also, and at the farther end we could count sixteen large beaver houses from our vantage point, but there was no activity anywhere. All life seemed to be content just to bask in the warm sunshine, and the lake itself was a still reflection of sky, clouds, and shoreline.

Just back of the point we found a spring that emptied into the bay. We were overjoyed at this discovery, for we now had a source of cold, sparkling water for drinking purposes, high land on which to fashion our Utopia among the twinkling birches, rocky shores to dive from into the deep water, all right at our door, plus seclusion, and apparently game and fur aplenty. We lost no time in carrying our exploration further, and in the late afternoon completely circled the lake by canoe.

There were new phenomena to arouse our interest every day, and this one was no exception. Down the lake in the direction of the beaver colony, there was a block-wide swath in the timber where the tallest and largest trees, great hemlocks that stood above the surrounding hardwood, were all broken off about halfway up their length, leaving gaunt, barkless stubs with only one or two larger branches, broken likewise, sticking out from the trunks like the arms of scarecrows. It must have been the path of a terrific tornado, which, like a reaper's scythe, had years before clipped off the protruding tops of these forest giants as though they were toothpicks.

As we paddled along, we flushed a pair of wood duck that took off and landed on the branches of the stubs, bobbing their heads on long, inquisitive necks at our intrusion. These large birds, graceful in flight or on the water, looked comically awkward roosting in trees. I noticed that nearly all the stubs had holes in them where branches had rotted off. The holes were larger than those I had so often seen occupied by a family of woodpeckers or flickers, and as I watched, a merganser winged in and lit in true woodpecker style on the side of one of them, his webbed feet hooked over the edge of the opening. I never knew before that ducks were that agile and nested in hollow trees, but this windswept section proved to be a duck rookery of exclusive skyscraper apartments.

We now had a new source of supply for eggs that lasted about a month. The female duck lays about twelve to fourteen eggs for a setting and will not give up on filling her nest. As regularly as possible, we relieved our duckery of the surplus, keeping a close record and stopping when we had taken thirty eggs from any one nest. This margin of safety invariably ensured a full, if rather belated, hatch of spring ducklings.

A pair of osprey had built in the very top of one of the taller stubs that had three supporting branches on which the nest rested. It was an old established penthouse, nearly eight feet in diameter and three feet deep at the trunk. I first noticed one of the birds as we came up the lake. He was wheeling on motionless wings in great circles far up in the cloudless blue sky. Suddenly he folded like a duck that has been perfectly centered with a charge of fine shot from a hunter's gun and plummeted toward the water with the speed of a rocket. When he struck, the spray flew four feet in the air. He had completely submerged and I thought he must surely be mortally wounded from the force of the impact, but presently he surfaced and arose empty-taloned. We were much closer now, and he made several anxious circles over the spot where he had struck, peeping plaintively like a lost chick in a hen yard. "Pheuw, pheuw, pheuw," he repeated over and over again, and then sailed off to perch disconsolately beside his nest, where he continued his lament with single "pheuws" at regularly spaced intervals. There was a slight disturbance in the water ahead of us, and we came upon about a five-pound northern pike, his head almost out of water, mouth wide open, pushing himself along with feeble flips of his fins. We could not determine whether he was completely out of commission or temporarily stunned, but left him in hopes that the osprey would return for the fruits of his spectacular high dive.

About a week later, we visited the stub where the osprey nested and from a rise discovered two scrawny necks covered with yellow down stretching up inquiringly, supporting flat, wide heads from which protruded cruel hooked beaks and glittering, intrepid eyes that glared belligerently down upon us. Both parents were very much perturbed, but we were only interested in the size of the nest and its construction. There were branches woven tightly together, some an inch and a half in diameter, and we could pick out each year's layer of added material by the weathered condition of the wood.

We were amazed at the conical pile of disintegrated fish bones circling the base of the tree. It was fully seven feet high and twice that in diameter. Except for the more recent waste, the bones were a rust-colored earthy material with only a few skull and backbone fragments to indicate the origin of the deposit. I thought of what a potent fertilizer this would make for the flower garden in Mother's yard back home.

At the beaver houses, we found short lengths of freshly peeled popple that indicated occupancy, and we sighted one old fellow sneaking away silently under the alders, hardly rippling the water as he quickly made for cover. Safe in the shadows, he hit the water with a resounding slap of his tail in warning to others of the colony that might have been abroad in the presence of danger.

On the farther shore, we threw out a hook and line and caught northern pike almost as fast as we could haul them in, great strapping fellows that weighed well over twenty pounds. This was disappointing, as we had hoped for walleyes or lake trout because of their finer eating quality and fewer bones.

Directly across from our birch point, there was a heavy stand of tall Norways, and we could visualize a log cabin made from the trunks of these straight, slender trees. We ran ashore and prospected our find, marking the straightest trees which could be felled to land in the lake. In this manner there would be no skidding problem to further tax our strength in getting our material to the water.

At the lower end of the lake, not visible from our campsite, we found the outlet, a small stream winding around through marsh, sparsely dotted with spruce. Here, lying around on the bog in the hush of evening, we counted eleven deer forced to take refuge in the cool soothing water from the flies and ticks that tortured them. Their bodies were completely submerged, but every head was alert, questioning the advisability of flight from our invasion of their retreat. There is an unwritten law, or ethic, among those who live in the interior, that it is within the rights of man to kill for food. Woodsmen are very conscious of this prerogative and never take more than they can consume. Only male animals are killed, and in warm weather all parts are preserved by salting, smoking, or drying, so that nothing is wasted. It is considered good hospitality to serve even the rangers and wardens going their rounds a juicy venison or moose steak, out of season, for they live as dangerously as the sourdough, and recognize the vicissitudes which make game laws impractical back in the wild country.

The fawns were still in their spotted coats, but we had been out of red meat for days and decided that we would replenish our meat supply. Further up on the creek we spotted a large fawn lying close to the bank, and shot it. I have never heard such a racket. The report of our rifle reverberated over the marsh, bounced off the timbered shores, and returned to us a hundredfold. Startled bitterns and long-legged cranes set up a terrific squawking and a group of nesting ravens in the clump of pines we had just passed took flight to investigate the disturbance, adding their croaking notes to the turmoil. It was fully ten minutes before the confusion subsided. Knee-deep in water, we dragged our prize back to the canoe. He was as round and fat as a butterball and about as hard to handle from the uncertain footing of a boggy floating marsh, but we loaded him aboard and headed for camp, following the shore-line en route to complete our investigation.

As we left the creek mouth, the water deepened rapidly, and we picked up some nice walleyes at the edge of a small bed of weeds. We were pleased to find that the lake harbored this more desirable fish as well as the northern; now we were assured quality eating in fish, fowl, and red meat and trap bait besides—right in our own lake. Our spirits soared to new heights as we landed and contemplated the site of our future abode, building a log castle in our minds to huge proportions.

The fawn supplied us with meat far beyond our estimation. We could not possibly consume more than the loins and haunches, even with our ravenous appetites, and it was with deep regret that we carried the balance of the animal back into the woods to be devoured by the carnivorous creatures that passed that way in the night. Venison chops and raw-fried potatoes made a very satisfying change in our diet.

We decided to finish packing everything of a permanent nature that we had in our outfit in the morning, and that evening we scuffed out in the soft earth a crude floor plan for our cabin among the birches. From now on it was a matter of hard labor, working against time, to provide ourselves with a focal point from which to continue our explorations in preparation for the fall trapping season and the long winter that, before many months had passed, we knew would close in upon us and completely cut us off from civilization. We brought in our tent on the first load and set it up beside our cabin site, cutting uprights and ridgepoles from strong young timber and securely staking down the side walls and the guy lines against the worst in storms that we could anticipate. On subsequent trips we brought in the rest of our dunnage, stacking it neatly in our tent, preparatory to traveling light on our return trip to town. The food we packed in a gunnysack, which we cached out of the sun high in the top of a spruce by throwing a rope over a branch and hauling it up beyond the reach of the tallest animal. This procedure lessened the chances of woods marauders tearing our packs to pieces in search of edible material among our belongings while we were gone.

Weary from our efforts, but in feverish haste, we crossed the portage again, cast off late in the day, and headed down the lakes for the village. Our memory served us well and though it was dark when we arrived, we managed by nightfall to make Saganaga Lake, where we had found the full rookery. We named the rookery Gull Island. A narrow point of land gave us an ideal campsite, with a cross breeze that minimized the mosquitoes, and after a hurried supper of fish steaks, roasted on green-forked sticks held over the coals of our fire, we slept peacefully, the water lapping gently against the shores on both sides of us. It took eleven days going in, but only four days coming out. It looked as though we had not gone far enough and were practically in town, but when we stopped to figure that it would take better than a week for a round trip, we did not anticipate many visits from the townsfolk, should our friends happen to find our hideaway.

Life in the village had gone on as usual, and it remained for us to purchase a rigid canoe to supplement our over-worked folding canvas model, to find building material for our cabin, and to complete our load with all the food our canoe caravan would hold. We took up our abode in what we now laughingly referred to as our four-dollar house, and after two days of shopping, going over lists, packing, repacking, and building for easy portaging, we were ready for the return trip. We had found a new lightweight eighteen-foot Old Town canoe that fitted our needs perfectly. There were rolls of tar paper, resin paper, roofing, complete windows, nails, screws, hinges, locks and bolts, carpenter's tools, rope, food, utensils, and clothing. The only thing we didn't load was the car, which was put up on blocks and locked in the garage for a well-earned rest. We had bought a good four-hole wood stove with an oven, but with some sign of momentary sanity, it was decided we could cook outdoors until fall, when the ice would afford us an easier method of transportation for this luxury.

Our alarm clock woke us at four. A big breakfast gave us strength for the coming ordeal, and our spirits buoyed our determination to get under way. We loaded and trimmed the two canoes and estimated the total weight of our supplies at around eighteen hundred pounds. There would be no sailing on Basswood Lake this trip, for our gunwales cleared the water by a scant three inches. There is no need to dwell on the labor, sweat, and toil of this back-breaking, spirit-crushing return journey. Suffice it to say that outside of the insects that attacked us continually, raising welts at our wrists and necklines, nature was kind to us. Our days were cool and sunny, our nights heavenly; gentle breezes that ruffled the water neither hindered nor helped our progress. Contrary to our expectations, we were again fortunate and did sail the full four-mile length of Basswood, not with surging charges astride spume-topped billows, but wafted gently along on little choppy wavelets that lapped softly at our prows. This was a welcome respite from our muscle-tiring miles of paddling, and we lounged contentedly on the thwarts in the sun, occasionally trailing a bare foot in the cooling waters as we sailed peacefully along.

On the point at Prairie Portage, where the creek empties into Basswood Lake over a sparkling twelve-foot falls, we had noticed the remains of a large Indian encampment. This grassy plain when we went down had been dotted with naked teepee poles and bent-over birch and alder skeletons of former wigwams, the ashes of abandoned family cooking fires with their bare ridge-poles from which to suspend the boiling kettles, and other minor evidences of previous activity. My guess had been that a fishing party had been seining the mouth of the river for spawning white fish. I was entirely wrong.

In the short space of three days, the camp had been completely rehabilitated. Teepees and summer houses were covered with bright new sheets of birch bark, decorated with designs and queer figures of man and beast, painted in bright new colors. The campfires were going and there was bustling activity throughout the camp. We learned on inquiry that the spring powwow was on in full force, and we decided to lay over for a day to see this annual pageant. The natives of the immediate area were the hosts, and guests arrived from other villages as far as four hundred miles away. How the participants, in their scattered retreats, received notice by the woodland grapevine of the time and place of the gathering is a mighty mystery to me, but there they were, at the appointed moment, taking part in the festivities. Primarily the meeting is called for the purpose of prayer and sacrificial offerings to the Indian gods, beseeching them to bring peace and prosperity to their tribes for the coming year. It is a period of feasting and performance of the peace dance. In these years of comparative civilization, it had revolved into more of a homecoming celebration, but many of the rites were still carried out in devout solemnity.

The men of the tribe were busy foraging for meat, the women preparing the meals, exchanging gossip, and tendering what hospitality the camp afforded. The visitors bring no food, but lavish presents of all kinds upon their hosts. Beadwork, knife sheaths, moccasins, belts, deerskin vests, mittens, feathered headdresses, necklaces, and other handiwork are but a few of the tokens of friendship.

The peace dance goes on continuously to the monotonous rhythm of the "tum tum—tum tum—tum tum" of the drums. Little Indian boys kneel at the fire, heating the heads of spare instruments, so that the skins are always dry and taut and give out a sharp resounding boom that quickens the feet of the dancers. The younger braves vie for honors and dance continuously night and day until they stumble and fall from complete exhaustion, at which point their friends and backers carry them off the scene. We found many of our Indian friends from the town and village at the powwow and were shyly invited to take part in the dance, which we did in a gesture of sport and friendship.

The dance floor was a well-worn circular path in the dust about twenty feet in diameter, enclosed by fresh-cut brush with openings on each side to receive the dancers. A small stage in one corner accommodated the drummers, and the participants circled in slow solemn motion, shuffling along in cadence with the drums, the invited dancers directly behind their partners. To engage a partner for a dance, some small token of esteem is proffered. If it is accepted, an exchange of tokens is effected and the couple joins the circling figures. Etiquette demands that the couple complete at least one round, after which anyone may cut in, or either dancer may drop out. In the center of the circle, the more exuberant male youngsters carried on a dance under the disapproving frowns of the elder members of the gathering.

A withered but tolerant old woman proffered me a short length of faded blue ribbon in a kindly gesture to assist us in lowering the bars of formality and diffidence with which the younger generation regarded us. I, in turn, unprovided with reciprocal favors, gave her a nickel in return. She instructed me in the proper movement and halting shuffle of the dance, which I proudly mastered to the satisfaction of the watchers in three turns of the ring. My partner then dropped out, and I repaired to the sidelines. The length of time it took the ancient one to tell that we were passing out money as favors was all that was required to make us the most popular dancers on the grounds among the old and young alike, and the nickels and dimes we offered disappeared immediately into the deep pockets hidden in the folds of the billowing skirts of our female companions. It was all we could do to reach a more comely member of the assembly, and one more to our liking, before a bolder and more avaricious oldster would pounce on us with anything from a needle to a used buckskin moccasin lacing. It was very amusing while it lasted, but the money never again turned up as a token, and we soon ran out of nickels and dimes. The hour was getting late and we had a big day ahead of us, so we retired to our own camp for the night.

Three days later we arrived at the long portage into Expectancy. Eighteen hundred pounds for two men through four miles of timber meant eleven trips apiece back and forth, so it was another three days before our belongings were all safely in camp. A hundred pounds is not a bad load to pack when it is compact and well balanced, but with many cumbersome, misshapen pieces it was a different problem. Our ardor had cooled considerably with these exertions, and there were signs that Corney was beginning to wonder whether the joys to come were worth the strenuous efforts of the present.

After resting for a day, swimming in the lake, sleeping and lolling about camp, we were back to work again. We cut and felled enough pine trees from the clump across the lake to build our cabin, sending them crashing into the water, where we cut them into eighteen- and twenty-two-foot lengths. Grouping the two separately into two rafts, we bound them with two cross poles nailed to the ends of the outer logs and reinforced the blocks with shorter branches at intervals on the deck of each raft. In the center, toward the front, we erected a short, stout mast and guyed this to all four corners. The rafts were anchored securely to the shore, and we returned to camp to prepare a skidway to the cabin site while awaiting a favorable wind to ferry our timber across the lake. We cut a ten-inch-thick popple into eighteen-inch lengths for rollers and laid and smoothed a pair of skids up the steep bank on which to roll the logs, for they would be heavy to handle at best.

One day we awoke to a spanking breeze coming directly in off the lake and knew this was our chance. Across the lake, we cast the rafts loose from their moorings, poled them out to where we could catch a breeze, and away we went, shouting and laughing like a couple of youngsters playing Captain Kidd or Robinson Crusoe, our blue army blanket, for the third time, doing passable duty as a sail. The rafts did not make time like our smooth-bottomed canoe, but the breeze stiffened to where we felt that we would reach shore by the middle of the afternoon. Steering by turn, we swam and dove from the raft as we crossed. In the middle of the lake, disaster overtook us, and our tow raft began to break up. We salvaged what we could by reinforcement but spent the greater part of the next day picking up the other logs that had drifted singly into shore. Now came the test as we struggled, groaned, and grunted these logs up the skidway, snubbing our line to a tree on the bank and blocking the log while we rested. Inch by inch, up they came. We hardly stopped to eat for fear the wind would rise and scatter the logs that still remained in the water in all directions before we could pull them to safety. Eventually the final log nosed slowly up the bank, and with a sigh of relief we rested the next two days by doing odd jobs that seemed to us like child's play after our improvised logging experiences.

We measured distances, dug grooves for the foundation logs, plotted our doors and windows, numbered our logs, starting with the larger, notching the ends so that each successive log would fit snugly along the entire length of the one before it. The first few logs were easy, but as the walls grew higher, it was more difficult to roll them up on skids placed on the top log and stop each in the right place to lodge securely into position.

It was now the twentieth of June, and I had begun to sense something wrong. Corney lay abed longer in the mornings. He grumbled about the work, the food, and the discomforts of camp life. He talked ceaselessly of city pleasures, ice cream sodas and malteds, and at times fairly made my mouth water. He spoke of dances, dates, and other city pastimes, and I began to fear the worst. I tried to put my finger on the cause of his displeasure and drove the harder to finish our cabin; I felt that, the hard work over, his spirits would revive with the renewal of our explorations.

One morning he would not get up at all, and out of pure cussedness, I threw back the mosquito bar and let in the army of waiting pests upon his prostrate form. I could hear him slapping and cursing as I worked on odd jobs that could be accomplished alone, and I chuckled at his discomfiture. This was the beginning of the end, I thought, for Corney was angry with me, and he moped and grumbled about camp all day. I didn't attempt to get him to help but left him to himself, hoping he would get back into good humor. For one who does not yearn for the outdoors, love the folk who live there, and revel in the beauties of nature, it is hard to understand why anyone would go through the hardships of wilderness life in order to obtain these joys. He cannot understand the willingness of man to sweat and toil, suffer inconveniences, forgo the so-called better things of life and culture, to be eaten up by insects, sleep on the hard ground, travel in the rain, and eat the simplest of fare.

Corney had entered into our agreement in the spirit of adventure and as a temporary diversion from which he could gain a thrill and some excitement, but to me it was all seriousness and life at its fullest, life without social demands, conflicts, or sophistication. There were no adjustments to make to cosmopolitan law and order; instinct and self-preservation alone governed our actions. There is no way to judge character without considering the social and animal aspects of man. We all suffer love, hope, fear, hunger, and despair, and all of us practice to a greater or lesser degree the survival of the fittest, for man is a selfish creature. We all seek happiness, and here in the outdoors I had found it. My greatest chore was a pleasure, my slightest experience a thrill.

The next morning, Corney was in a better frame of mind and apologized for his actions of the day before, and I begged for forgiveness for my lapse of consideration also, but he told me he couldn't take it any longer. I reminded him of our pact to stay a year, which he acknowledged, countering with the statement that he did not realize what it was like to be entirely on your own. To him the prize was not worth the effort. He felt that if he stayed longer he would lose all his self-respect. I pondered this statement for some time, but could only come to the conclusion that if a man never had any self-respect, he could not but gain some in such close communion with God's wild creatures and His handiwork. Was I wrong? Was I, too, losing my self-respect?

It finally occurred to me that he had to have a reason for quitting, and that, weak as it was, this was it. It was getting close to the Fourth of July. I imagined that that was what had been bothering him most. He could see the flags flying, the soldiers marching, the laughing, happy people milling about in this pageantry; he could hear the bands playing, too, calling him to come home. I do not blame him, for we were just cut from different pieces of cloth. I was the pioneer and adventurer and he the city boy. It was a body blow that tumbled my house of cards, or maybe I should say logs, down about my head. At any rate, I had to agree to go back also; there was nothing else I could do.

Once he had made his decision, Corney was so anxious to be done with it that he proposed to leave our entire outfit there in the woods to rot. It was worth well over two thousand dollars, but he refused to break camp and insisted on starting immediately, taking only the clothes on his back and sufficient provisions to see us into town. My conscience would not allow me to do this, and I determined to hire someone, if necessary, to go back with me and salvage what I could.

There were two routes to town from the border. The long way around, with four short portages, took longer but could be made by easy stages. The shorter route that would save a day's time entailed a single four-mile portage, used principally by the natives who lived in the Indian village at the far end and by those who traveled light, urgently needing some special item which could not be had short of the railroad settlement. We headed for the shortcut, arriving there about the middle of the afternoon. It was too late to make town that night, so we pitched camp alongside the trail, planning to take up the last lap of our journey in the morning. My spirits were very low, and I watched halfheartedly while some Indian children played games in the dust of the clearing.

A canoe drew up at the landing near where we had turned ours bottom side up for the night, and two men got out. One could tell by their methodical actions that they were practiced voyagers, for every movement counted. The tall one donned a packsack and with a smooth, effortless heave picked up the ninety-pound canoe out of the water and swung it into place, so that the padded thwart rested across his bony shoulders in a comfortable position. The short, stocky fellow picked up the other pack and the paddles with less alacrity, but with the natural easy swing of the woodsman, and they started up the trail in single file. As they came closer, it was apparent that the little man was old, the taller one under middle age. They were dressed in lightweight, bleached-out khaki-colored cotton shirts and breeches, damp and stained with perspiration. The tall one's shirt was a remnant from a ragbag, worn through at the elbows, the pocket hanging limply where it had ripped halfway from its seams. There was another rent over the shoulder blade that exposed a three-inch triangle of lean, browned skin under which long, firm muscles rippled easily. You could not immediately comprehend their faces. The upper halves were almost black, as though they had come in close contact with charred timber. Through this covering, little veins of bronzed and sun-reddened skin were visible where beads of sweat had trickled down their cheeks and temples, to be absorbed in their three weeks' growth of beard.

"Hi" was their greeting. Their eyes roved over our persons and encampment in all-seeing glances that took in the situation to their satisfaction, and as if by a command, they set down their burdens.

I was not so sure that I welcomed the company of these questionable characters; to say the best, they were a disreputable-looking pair. The old man sat down. By way of conversation, the tall one asked bluntly, "Heading in or out?"

"Out!" I replied.

They vouchsafed the information that they had been back in the brush for three weeks and during the morning had packed through recently burned-over country that had been green when they went in. This accounted for their unwashed appearance.

"What do you say, Jim?" asked the tall one.

The old man's reluctance to rise in itself was answer enough to the question, but he grumblingly replied, "Let's wait and make it tomorrow. There ain't no hurry, and besides, we got company now."

Introductions were in order, and I explained our being on the portage and my reluctance to curtail the holiday. The tall one, Bill Berglund, a guide from the village, had hired out to accompany "Jasper" Jim O'Niel [O'Neal],* the old one, into the iron country. Jim was eighty years old, and the trip was telling on him. In an aside from Bill, I learned that Jim had been a prospector in the territory forty years ago, and had yearned for one last look at the site of his operations. Trappers had kept up the old cedar log cabin that looked out across the lake at an outcropping of iron-bearing slate, so that it appeared much as Jim had remembered it in the past. In his childishness, Jim insisted that he was staying and wanted to die in the place he had so long ago called home. Bill tried to talk him out of it, and the present strained relationship was the result of his finally being forced to threaten to tie Jim up and forcibly place him in the canoe if he refused to go back.

The men pitched their tent alongside ours, washed up in cold lake water as well as could be expected, and suggested we pool our resources for supper. Bill seemed preoccupied, but Jim boasted of his prowess as a sourdough as we threw the meal together. They provided the staples and some very delicious biscuits while we supplied the vegetables and trimmings. As we chatted during the meal, Bill turned to me as if he had suddenly made up his mind to something and asked, "What would you want to do if you stayed on in the bush?"

I replied that I had no special plans other than to explore the border country, fish and enjoy life in general, and trap, if I stayed for the winter.

He thought for a minute, then said, "I'll go with you."

* Cook is probably referring, here and below, to the man listed in the 1920 census as James O'Neal, age 87, living in Winton, St. Louis County.

"What do you mean?" I queried.

"Well, I won't be doin' much till fall, and I'd kinda like to do the same thing, scoutin' some trappin' territory and maybe see some of the big lakes."

I had to think this one over. One minute I felt as though he had been sent to my rescue. The next minute I thought, "What if this character is some cold-blooded murderer hiding out in this vastness away from the law, who would think nothing of slitting my throat in the night just to obtain possession of our expensive equipment?" The wolves and bears would do away with my remains, and back home they would never know what had happened to me!

I had heard a tale in town of a big, surly Irishman living north of the border that I remembered reading about in the Minneapolis papers. His name was Butch Conway, or something like that. He had murdered his wife and evaded imprisonment by hiding in the Canadian wilderness. The story goes that he sent Indians in for his supplies, always went armed, and avoided the beaten trails and all contacts with the white population. There was no doubt in my mind that such a person existed, for I had met several trappers who claimed to have run across him in their travels.

When the dishes were done, I sauntered over to one of the larger buildings in the settlement where a mixed-blood, Leo Chosa,* carried a small stock of tobacco and supplies, and as an opening bought a can of beans. He was a friendly, talkative fellow, and I casually made inquiry about Bill and

---

* The 1920 census lists Leo Chosa, age thirty-seven and a trapper, living with his wife, Annie, age thirty-one, plus four daughters and one son in Winton, St. Louis County.

immediately got the history of his past. I explained my desire to team up with him, and Leo declared, "He's the orneriest bullheaded Swede that ever lived. The devil himself couldn't get along with him unless he had his own way all the time." I learned, however, that he was honest and well thought of in the community, even though they all considered him an incurable introvert. He had formerly worked in the sawmill; his wife had recently died in a flu epidemic, and since that time, grieving over his loss, Bill had quit his job and drawn farther and farther into himself, earning a meager living by trapping in winter and guiding spasmodically in summer. I had made one bad mistake, but if we could get along, an alliance with Bill would suit my purposes perfectly, and I went back and agreed to a trial partnership.

Our chance meeting changed plans for both Bill and me. First, we sorted out our equipment and left a bulging packsack with Leo. The items I had found to be non-essential on my first foray we took on back into town. The next day, Corney and I shook hands and he boarded the train for civilization, evening gowns, movies, sodas, milling crowds, tall buildings, hard pavements, autos, golf clubs, offices, paychecks, and drudgery. Jim O'Niel returned disconsolately to his boarding house, and Bill moved his belongings over to the town house where our new life began.

We PLANNED TO START IMMEDIATELY and pick up the equipment left at the cabin site on Lake Expectancy, bring it to town, pick out the necessities for light travel, store the balance at the town house against the possibilities of a more permanent arrangement later on, and be gone.

The first and most gratifying thing that I noticed after my new connection was the friendly greetings and change in attitude of both the white- and the red-skinned natives. I was no longer an outsider, watched with furtive, distant glances. I was one of them, a member of the community and a sourdough. The Indians, instead of maintaining an aloof silence, greeted me and conversed in understandable if not good English. Apparently, with all of them I had earned my right to a place in their midst. Leo owned a small launch on the first lake, which he used for hauling fish he bought from the Indians to an ice plant in town, where he packed them for shipment to market. He had graded up a right-of-way on the four-mile portage over which he drove a dilapidated Ford to the Indian village, where he ruled over his full-blood brothers as king, confidant and adviser. In summer, vacationers paid four dollars a head for ferrying and transporting of equipment across this private thoroughfare into Basswood Lake. We residents rode free and saved a full day's portaging and paddling into the bargain.

At Expectancy, Bill pooh-poohed the game possibilities and told me that Indians had killed off most of the moose and trapped out the beaver in that location long ago. Traveling overland, they could short-cut our route to about forty-five miles, just a good day's travel on snowshoes from their village,* and I wondered why I had not noticed this on the maps before. I said good-bye to the framework on our cabin, now up eight logs high, and in sorrow left the fruits of our back-breaking labors behind, never to return again.

We had agreed to go halves on everything, and I turned over to Bill a very fine new sleeping bag and a complete outfit of practically new clothing left behind by Corney in his rush to reach home by the Fourth of July. Bill was as proud and self-conscious as a kid with his first long breeches, even though his bony wrists did stick out of his new sleeves an inch too far, and he clung to his sleeping bag with the loving care of a little girl with her first mama doll.

Back in town, we stowed our duffel and Bill insisted we get out the flivver and make a trip to the county seat to find what areas were still open on which we could apply for a trapping permit. This could have been done at any time, but I soon ferreted out the real reason for the trip. His fingers itched to get at the wheel of the flivver. Bill wanted to learn to drive.

When we were out on the gravel highway,† I delivered a lecture on the intricacies of power-driven vehicles, stopped, started, backed up, and went forward for his benefit. He knew marine engines, so it was not necessary to go into mechanics, other than the steering mechanism. Finally I thought I had him all primed and turned over the wheel. He started off

* Traveling forty-five miles per day on snowshoes would require prodigious effort.
† Cook and Berglund probably traveled the primitive road from Ely to the Lake County seat at Two Harbors.

admirably, speeded up the motor and got into high in good shape, and down the road we went, faster and faster. The first indication I had that all was not well was that we were veering slowly toward the left side of the road. The faster we went, the harder he tramped on the accelerator; the more we veered to the left, the more pressure he put in that direction on the steering wheel. We were heading straight for the muck and slime of a big slough on the side of the road at forty miles per hour, and Bill's hands were frozen tightly to the wheel. I twisted it with all my strength as we hopped over some fresh grading, and I yelled at Bill to let go just as our wheels commenced to sink in the soft, swampy shoulder of the road.

We probably would have been in that mud hole yet, with just our top showing, if my shout had not brought Bill to his senses. Our axle plowed up the slime as I finally gained control of the wheel and twisted it back toward the road. The thick mire blacked out our windshield and I could not tell for a moment whether we would make it or not. It was a good thing we were going as fast as we were, for the light car skittered along on the pan over the surface of the slough like a flat stone on water, careened sharply to the right and stalled, just as our momentum brought us back to firm ground. Bill was trembling like a leaf and complained, "It went the wrong way."

"You're telling me," I retorted, after taking a deep breath. It dawned on me then that the only previous steering Bill had ever done had been on a launch with uncrossed rudder lines where it is necessary to turn the steering wheel to the left to cause the boat to make a right-hand turn, a very common hookup on marine craft. I laughed in my relief as Bill moved over and I resumed the driver's seat; he was cured, and from then on I was captain of the ship whenever we were on dry land.

At the county seat we stopped in at the conservation department, made out our applications for trapping permits, and were assigned the two border townships which we had hoped to obtain. This good fortune gave us the base on which to form our plans for winter, and with that in mind we spent the afternoon prowling the hardware and sporting goods shops to see what we could find. They were full of every imaginable device for the welfare, convenience, and comfort of the camper, and unlike in the city stores that display the gadget, the gaudy, and the eye-catching luxuries so dear to the heart of the tenderfoot, the merchandise as a whole had practical usage. I did buy a beautiful six-pound, sport-weight double-bitted ax that proved its worth many times over during the coming months. It was easy to pack and I kept it lashed to the back of my packsack, where it was accessible at every stop for such jobs as cutting firewood, tent poles and pegs, boughs for our beds, campfire stakes, trap drags, frozen fish for bait, and popple saplings to bait beaver sets, chopping holes in the ice for water or for trap sets, and for cutting out traps that had frozen in, cutting up game, trail blazing, and many other everyday tasks. I didn't shave with it, simply because I didn't shave while in the brush, although I kept one blade sharpened to a razor's edge at all times. It was my prize possession. Our shopping and business completed, we decided we were safer in the woods than in a man-made infernal machine called a flivver, and preferred to be on our way.

The next day I dropped my role as teacher and became a student, under the able instruction of my new sourdough partner. We had flapjacks for breakfast, and what cakes they were. Bill's magical witches' caldron of sourdough, on occasion, yielded the most varied and delectable selection of breadstuffs that you could imagine—flapjacks, buckwheat cakes, cornmeal pancakes, corn bread, sourdough bread, biscuits, dough gods, muffins, bannock, and many other masterpieces of camp cookery.

The basic ingredients of this manna-producing concoction are flour and water, to which a souring agent such as yeast or vinegar has been added. This forms the nucleus around which the expert builds his end products, varying his fare from day to day by changing the ingredients he adds to the mixture. A cupful or more of the material is always held over as a primer for use in starting the next batch, and I have heard old-timers boast that their sourdough had been working constantly for periods upwards of ten years. Certainly the odors which arise from these stench pots verify their claims.

Another and probably the most vital function of the sourdough pail is its ability to absorb, without changing character, all of the scraps from the table that might otherwise be wasted. These disintegrate through the fierce action of the live yeast cells that feed on the contents, and some braggarts will soberly and proudly claim that their particular brand will absorb a boot heel, even to the nails, overnight.

When you leave the beaten trails on a long trip and know your only source of supply for months will be your packsack, selection of the bare necessities of life and their conservations become a serious matter. One mistake or omission can be of dire consequence and bring untold misery and discomfort on your entire journey. Likewise, overzealousness can be the cause of many unnecessary, back-breaking trips on the many portages. Balance and weight are the watchwords, and the wise traveler strips down like a channel swimmer for his wilderness wanderings.

We prepared our flour in advance, mixing in the proper proportions of salt, sugar, and baking powder. To make a batch of biscuits, it was then only necessary to add shortening, pour the required amount of water into a depression in the sack of flour, mix, and remove the resulting ball of dough. The balance of the flour then remained dry and was ready for flapjacks, bannock, or more biscuits at the next meal.

There are as many cups of beverage in a pound of tea as there are in four pounds of coffee. We drank tea. The other main items of food consisted of slab bacon, dried fruit, rice, oatmeal, seasoning, and butter. It is next to impossible to eliminate all angular objects that cut into your back on the portages, but as much as possible we repacked the dry items into small sacks rather than leave them in original tins and cartons. I marveled at many of these little weight- and space-saving economies. Our butter we placed in a tight, press-top can, for which we made a thick burlap container that could be kept wet by dipping it in the lake at intervals. Evaporation of the wet covering kept the contents cool enough to prevent running in the warmest weather.

Our utensils narrowed down to a boiling pot, frying pan, tea pail, biscuit pan, sourdough container, plates, cups, knives, forks, spoons, and the one luxury we allowed ourselves, a reflector baker. The usefulness of our baker, except on forced trips, outweighed the disadvantages of its weight and varied our fried diet with an occasional roast of meat or baked fish.

All of our duffel stowed away into three packsacks in addition to our canoe and paddles. One contained a change of clothing, first aid, repair kit, heavy cord, whetstone, oil, marine glue, and other odds and ends for our comfort and convenience, as well as our cooking utensils. Another was crammed to the brim with groceries, our sleeping bags and tent making up the third. Axes were securely lashed to the backs of the packs, and Bill carried a holstered, long-barreled twenty-two-caliber revolver, and our case knives hung from our belts. With supplies sufficient to carry us for sixty days, packs on our backs, the canoe suspended over our heads between us, we could make the portages in one trip, hardly losing a stride on the crossings. By now, I was a hardened veteran and handled my share of the load with ease.

The first of our route lay over much the same ground I had covered earlier. We stayed overnight at the Indian village and visited with some of the strangest characters I had ever met: Frank Chosa, a surly mixed-blood trapper and brother to Leo who ran the trading post; Joe Bushaw,* another trapper with alcoholic tendencies married to an Indian woman; and Joe Pete, Chippewa Indian, and his wife and two daughters, one named Pauline, a Chippewa maiden with a college education.† Many of these Indians were well educated and, I had heard, very wealthy. They had sold large government

* The 1920 census lists a Joseph Buchard, age fifty-six, a trapper living in Fall Lake Township, Lake County.
† The 1920 census lists a Joseph Peat, age fifty-six, living with his wife, Mary, forty-five, and eight children in Fall Lake Township, Lake County.

land grants to the lumber companies and received monthly remittance checks from the Indian agent who looked after them and doled out sufficient money for their needs. I met Walk-Up-the-Hill, a seamed- and leathery-faced woman of indeterminable age. She was a friendly, tolerant individual, grown wise with her many years of woods life, who took delight in recounting fishing and trapping experiences that added greatly to my knowledge of the ways of the creatures of the wild.

I learned later that Bill was seriously considering marrying an Indian woman. He missed his dead wife terribly and had wandered the woods like a lost soul since her departure. The object of his affections, a tall, stately Indian spinster, had the rather masculine, but interesting, name of Jack Rabbit. She was a fine woman with a high school education that, at least, placed her on a plane with Bill's eighth-grade attempt at learning. She was reported to have in trust with the government some seventy-five thousand dollars that brought her a comfortable monthly remittance check. I don't mean to infer that Bill's eye was on the money. He was just plain lonely and needed companionship of a sort that could stand up to the rugged type of life he proposed to lead. I am sure she looked on his bashful courtship with favor, and I often wonder whether or not a marriage was consummated in later years.

With the exception of a mongrel dog, which I foolishly fed scraps from our breakfast, the village was not yet awake when we pushed off from shore and left behind the last established vestige of civilization that we were to see for over a month. The Indian and the experienced woodsman use a short, fast-tempo paddle stroke that brings into play the muscles of the back as well as the arms, dividing the expended effort between the two, thereby causing less fatigue when traveling by canoe. The body sways forward and backward with the stroke and it is not necessary to extend the arms but slightly to put full power into the paddle, and the next stroke begins before the water drag has had an opportunity to appreciably slow up the forward motion of the canoe. I had to learn to paddle all over again to keep in rhythm with Bill. An informed observer can identify the novice as far as the eye can distinguish the occupants from the canoe itself, and the difference in acceleration is quite noticeable.

Some thirty miles from the village I discovered our Indian dog following us along the shore. To discourage him, we lunched on an island at noon, but when we landed that night, some fifty-five miles distant, there he was, skulking in the bushes as we pitched camp. Much against my principles of kindness toward dumb animals, we did not feed him, and were careful to stow our provisions securely before retiring. Nevertheless, in the morning, one of our packsacks had been chewed open, ruining it, and a full slab of bacon, dog and all, were gone. This taught me a lesson as regards half-starved dogs, whose very existence depends on their cunning and trickery.

We were well on our way and entering the territory we proposed to trap in the fall. Here we left the traveled routes of the border and turned north on an obscure and difficult chain of heavily timbered lakes running up into Canada. They were beautiful, lying in deep shadow from the lofty conifers that line their shores. The spring-fed, clear, cold waters teemed with delicious lake trout and walleyed pike. We nearly foundered that night on two five-pounders filleted and baked alongside the coals of our campfire.

This was otter country, and our purpose was to investigate the fifth lake of the chain, which had several known beaver-dammed inlets. The lake was called Ottertrack Lake; in some prehistoric time, a mammoth otter had left a trail of footprints six inches in diameter on an inclined mudbank that, through the ages, had solidified into stone and clearly retained these inch-deep impressions in the face of the rock. It was hard to visualize a freshwater otter of a size big enough to leave those impressions.

We scouted the creeks for several days. One late afternoon, we came out on a rocky promontory that ended the ridge we were following. Directly below us and connecting with the continuation of our ridge on the farther side was a large beaver dam. We sat down for a smoke and contemplated the work of these little creatures who built with such intelligence and ingenuity. We could see where they had first felled giant popple from each bank into the cut through which the stream had formerly passed unhampered. They then felled smaller trees in back of the large ones to fill up the gap, and floated down countless thousands of short lengths of timber which they wove into an intricate pattern with stones, grasses, and mud to block the passage of the water.

While we sat there motionless, I noticed a faint succession of concentric ripples emanating from a few spears of grass in the center of the pond. Watching closely, I cautioned Bill in a whisper not to move, and finally could make out a nose and one bright little eye, perfectly still, peering out between the blades of grass. There were no signs of movement, but slowly the whole head appeared and then the top of the body followed. The beaver looked all around carefully and with only a ripple pushed out into the pond, where another complete survey was made. He seemed to be satisfied and dove back down under the water. In possibly a minute, he reappeared near the house with a load of mud, stone, and small twigs which he carried in his forearms. Standing erect and balancing on his broad tail, he waddled up the side of the house and deposited his load, stamping it into position on the house with his hind feet. He dove down again, and his reappearance seemed to be the signal for the rest of the family to come forth also, as four more appeared in quick succession. One of the group headed directly for the dam and made a thorough inspection of its full length. The water was a little high, and without further ado, he enlarged the opening through which there was already a trickle of water escaping. Two of the others struck off upstream while the other two dove again and brought up more material for the house. They then followed the first two, and we could hear them cutting popple in a grove along the bank about thirty yards away.

When the keeper of the dam finished his job, he climbed the bank directly opposite us, and we watched him struggle with a four-foot length of popple fully eight inches in diameter which he was dragging down one of their skidways. The log was as big as he was, and I believe weighed slightly more than he did. He pulled on a protruding nub of a limb and rocked the log slowly. It gave a few inches. He braced himself on a root and got a better purchase. The log moved about a foot but lodged behind the root that had been a help the moment before. It moved a few inches more. Now he was logging. He braced himself behind a stump with feet and tail, and with each audible grunt the log moved down the skidway by as much as its own length. It was evident that beaver do not help each other, but they seem never to tackle a job they are unable to handle alone. This old lumberjack had his hands, feet, and tail full, but he was evidently accomplishing his purpose. We watched him for an hour or more while he brought his timber to the water, but the sun was getting low and we had to leave. No doubt the heavy piece would lend support to some point in the dam that showed a weakness.

We circled the swamps, looking and recording in our memories locations for sets for mink, otter, beaver, fisher, muskrat, wolf, and fox when freezing weather that would prime the fur arrived in the fall. We had seen many signs of plentiful game, and I was thrilled and impatient to get under way, but there was still a lot to do before we would be in shape for winter.

We had been told of an old abandoned iron mine on Gunflint Lake, farther to the east of us, that Bill wished to visit. There was iron there, all right, but it had to be taken out by way of Canada and brought back down to the steel mills by such a circuitous route that the cost had been prohibitive. The present owners, a Chicago group, had turned it into a stock-selling project, buying the property a dozen times and selling it to the gullible people in the city with their visions of quick riches. When we got there, we were surprised to find a new promotion under way and a small crew working the shafts. We had supper and breakfast with them and inspected the shaft in the morning before going on to the far eastern end of the border chain.

At North Lake, Ontario, we found a lone enterprising backwoodsman who acted as postmaster and storekeeper for the Indian and white trappers of the area. In his leisure moments, he raised silver fox and fed them on fish he caught in his nets in the lake, and on deer he shot in the woods. He had a beautiful kennel of redbone hounds that he used in running the deer, and I was sorry we were not there in the fall to hear their deep, excited voices ringing through the woods as they coursed in full pursuit of their quarry.

Arrow Mountain,* Moose, and North and South Fowl Lakes ended the eastern chain. We stopped here and packed in to Partridge Falls on the Pigeon River, a two-day trip. It was a beautiful sight but a heartbreaking grind in the heat and insects of early August. We were glad to get back again to the cool lake breezes and easier travel by canoe and paddle. Planning a fast return, we trimmed our canoe carefully, consolidating our belongings into fewer packs and keeping out only the necessities.

The mine was our first overnight stop. This time we met the two sons of the promoter. They were apparently heartily disliked by the crew because of their arrogant manner, and the foreman told us the boys planned on following us down in the morning, at the same time suggesting we lose them en route. They were afraid to ask permission to accompany us for fear we would demand a guiding fee, but sure enough, they were up early and intercepted us around the first point,

* Cook probably meant modern Rose Lake, which connects with Arrow Lake.

calmly taking up their position half a city block behind us in their canoe.

The portage out of Gunflint was an easy one and there was no reason for us to gamble and run the treacherous rock-strewn river, but we decided to lose the boys then and there. They appeared to be puzzled when we passed the trail and headed for the river, but came gamely on behind us. As we entered the outlet, the river plunged down ahead in a series of boiling white-water rips, and we were away with a swoosh. Bill, in the bow, warded us off the jagged rocks and I did my best in the stern to check our toboggan-like progress with my paddle. At times we scrambled into the bottom of the canoe, lying down flat to avoid being swept from our seats by the interlacing alders that reached out for us from both banks, not two feet over the water, like the flailing arms of a giant octopus. We had almost mastered the fast water when a sound as of a sharp knife cutting through paper rose above the slap of the ripples. There was no jarring of the canoe that would indicate contact with a submerged obstacle, but water spouted in from below in tiny geysers. The point of rock had sliced through the painted canvas hull as keenly as a razor blade. This was probably our pay for being so inhospitable to our uninvited guests, but we made it to shore without soaking our belongings and hid in the bushes to watch the fun when the other canoe came through. After a half-hour wait, we gave up and pitched camp. The next day was spent in repairing a three-foot slit in the canvas bottom of our craft. We dried out the boat thoroughly before a huge fire, filled the rent with a mixture of hot spruce pitch and rosin, and glazed over the surface with a thin coating of commercial canoe glue that made us almost as good as new again. We had lost a whole day.

An early start the next morning landed us late in the afternoon on Knife Lake, a particularly beautiful one, with long wooded points sticking out into the water where we had camped before and where we had a good chance of picking up another succulent trout for our supper. After pitching the tent, we trolled the shore until almost dusk and were about to give it up as a bad job when Bill landed a big one. As we were eating, another canoe entered the lake with a solitary figure in the stern. He skirted the opposite shore and pulled in opposite our camp. We were puzzled. He did not paddle like an Indian—in fact, we thought of the boys we had eluded—but the lone voyager built an Indian-style fire that gave out the merest flicker of light across the lake and then went out. When this happened twice, our curiosity got the best of us and we slipped across in our canoe.

One of the boys from the mine bent over a sickly smudge, fanning it with his hat, trying at the same time to broil a small piece of fish impaled on a pointed stick. They had attempted the river also and overturned in the first rapids, losing all of their belongings. The less adventurous one had returned to the camp on foot, but the boy at the fire had determined to go on through. He was wet and shivering, and very much subdued. It made us feel ashamed of our part in the catastrophe, so we invited him across to a hot meal and dry bed, for which he was thankful. During the next day, he learned many things that opened his eyes to the ease and comfort of woods travel under experienced methods. Robbed of his superiority, he wasn't a bad fellow at all, and became quite friendly. We sped him on his way the next morning with full instructions on the route to town and enough food to last him through the trip. He wanted to pay us then, but we were glad to make amends for our lack of kindliness on leaving the mines.

Our program was now pretty well in mind, and we had settled on three locations from which to carry on our winter's activities. For our headquarters camp, we picked a rather large abandoned board shanty, the only building still standing of an old logging camp at the head of Iron Mountain Lake.* It had been the office. Among the ruins, we found an old camp cookstove that was almost beyond repair. The grates were burned out, the oven rusted through on all sides, and the top and lids cracked in every direction. If we could find what we wanted in town, we decided it could be put in shape to last another winter, so we took careful measurements, listed what we needed to repair the stove and shack, and the additional food supplies we would need, and headed back to civilization.

The trip was uneventful. At the old sawmill in the village, we found plenty of usable sheet iron and a discarded grate from one of the steam boilers which we cut in two to make a grate for the stove and a spare as well; they would do the work nicely. Some rolls of heavy tar paper for the outside, and some resin paper, salvaged from the unfinished cabin on Lake Expectancy, to seal the inside, would make our abode very comfortable, and we loaded the canoe to its limit with this material and additional food for a more permanent camp, and returned.

* No lake with this name exists today.

The shack was located on a high point of solid rock that jutted out into the narrows at the juncture of four lakes. We could see water in all directions from our windows and hear the pleasant music of a small falls hidden from our view by a birch-covered spit of land across the lake from us. The logging company had blasted out a cellar in the solid rock and built the building over it. Here we had a wonderfully cold yet dry depository for all of our perishables, which kept them from freezing even during the bitter cold of midwinter. It was a vantage point from every angle. We had easy access to the village for supplies, and each lake was a waterway into the wilderness country where we would establish our traplines.

Looking out of the entrance to this headquarters lodge, you gazed onto a hill with water on each side of it. It was around eighty feet high, with a long grassy slope running almost to our door, dotted with occasional clumps of young white birch, popple, and other small bushes. Halfway up the hill wound a well-worn deer trail used by these animals in skirting the height as they followed the waterways in their travels. Every night just at dusk, a large doe stopped in full view of the cabin and stared down at the light in our window. We always kept a rendezvous with her when we were at home, and would not have been a minute off had we set our watches by her appearance. We saw many more deer on this trail, and I learned that the grassy hillside, where low brush, clover, and timothy offered excellent grazing, was a favorite feeding ground for them. In the spring, the deer fed there in large numbers when forage in the wooded areas was still scarce.

We used Jim O'Niel's cedar log cabin as our second home.

Here was a fine frost-proof root house tunneled into the hill-side, and the premises and stove were in good repair. There was a living room, a bedroom with two double-tiered pole bunks, a kitchen, and a lean-to woodshed as well as a fine porch with a good view of the lake. The lean-to was almost full of empty gallon crockery jugs. The occupants must have put great faith in the curative powers of whiskey, whatever their ills, for there were no poisonous snakes or reptiles in the area unless you could count the ones seen through the glazed eyes of those who, themselves, had visited the jugs too frequently. In contrast to this earthy indication of a rugged life, we found old letters written in a fine hand on beauti-fully engraved stationery and postmarked Milan, Italy, from the wife of one of O'Niel's partners, offering him courage and devotion as she toured the watering places of the Old World during his long adventuresome explorations in the iron country. The explorer's cabin was an incongruous set-ting for epistles that suggested winding staircases, great halls, and drawing rooms with maid and butler service.

We had to build our third stopover shelter ourselves. It was constructed of light poles chinked with moss and roofed over with sod that barely cleared our heads. You could lie in the built-in bunk across one end and feed the fire in the round oak heater in the far corner without arising. We did no inside cooking here, as it was primarily a stopover when the day's work prevented us from making one or the other of our more permanent camps.

During the season, we picked and canned one hundred eighty pints of wild blueberries and ninety pints of wild raspberries, and put up another one hundred containers of preserves and jelly. The wild fruits were far superior to the domesticated varieties, and I drool now as I remember the blueberry pie, the chokecherry jelly, and the wild strawberry jam that we feasted on throughout the long winter.

Later, at each shack, we cut small quantities of pitch pine and dry cedar for kindling, and split and corded up to dry against the rigors of winter huge piles of beautiful green-body maple and birch that make my back ache as I think of them now.

Everything was now ready, except for the last-minute preparations that must necessarily wait until after the freeze-up, and we had nearly a month left to play. I awaited the first snow as anxiously as a kid with a new sled. Our labors had steeled my muscles so that my thighs would almost turn the blade of an ax, and my biceps and forearms swelled with long rippling fibers that would put to shame the circus strong man. I had never been in better physical condition. We had not had a visitor in all this time to break the monotony of our long work period, and hankered for company and news of the world, so we planned to run into town for a well-earned vacation.

The next day broke dull and expectant, and dark ominous clouds skudded across the sky, fanned by gusty bursts of high wind. The lake fairly danced with choppy little seas, scurrying here and there, bumping into each other, undecided as to which direction to take in their flight. We thought we could make it and started for the first portage, the wind buffeting our canoe and the cold spray taking our breath away. Across the portage lay my old bugaboo, Basswood. It didn't look too bad, and we were halfway down its length when the weather man finally decided what to do. The wind settled into the northwest and increased in fury, accompanied by short squalls and torrents of rain that completely obscured our vision. We were soaked to the skin. The waves at times reached nearly four feet, and we were taking water over the bow continuously as the crests broke in front of us. There was only one thing we could do, and we turned tail and ran before them, surging along on the crests and wallowing in the troughs. At a spot on shore almost directly in front of us that looked less rocky than the rest, we ran full on into the breakers. As we were about to round, we jumped out one on each side and hoisted the canoe clear out of the water without taking in a single roller, a technique I had perfected on the first run under sail down this same lake with my former partner. We had timed it just right. The wind shifted rapidly into the northeast, and we knew we were in for more rain and a real blow.

For the moment we were too busy finding a sheltered location for our tent and getting up between squalls to take stock of our surroundings. When all was under cover, to our surprise we saw another camp about seventy-five yards down the shore, but then it poured so hard we dined on cold biscuits and partridge and went to bed, leaving the investigation of the other travelers for the morning.

Our tent shook loose in the night and, in turn, bulged and collapsed with noisy slapping reports that awoke us soon after daylight. We tightened down everything and breakfasted on flapjacks, bacon, and coffee. Skuds of mist smashed in off the water, the sky was sullen, and the wind blew harder than ever, but it had stopped raining, so we decided to make our call. Our neighbors were not aware of our presence until we walked into their camp, as they were snugly under cover when we landed and a slight rise and some bushes hid our tent from their view. They had a nice outfit. There was a new White featherweight canoe and a seven-by-nine silkolene tent with outside ties put up in true expert fashion without a wrinkle on its entire surface, a job that put to shame our hurried preparations of the night before. The men were Canadian rangers on border patrol, also marooned by the storm, and Bill was pleasantly surprised to find Jack Powell and his son, old friends that we had planned to visit on our return home, their place being twenty-eight miles above ours.* The third man was a tall, reserved, scholarly looking stranger who had recently been assigned to the patrol with Jack. His name was Archie Covington, apparently an Englishman, and I immediately took a liking to him, for he seemed to be my kind.

Bill had told me that Powell lived with an Indian woman, which accounted for his son Mike's coppery skin and Indian features. Jack had come into the territory as a lumberjack twenty years before our chance meeting. Shortly afterwards, an alliance with a young Indian girl had resulted in her presenting him with a daughter in the spring of that same year. He had built a cabin at the logging camp and she, matter-of-factly, moved in and took over the family chores, cooking their meals and doing the washing and mending. It was not a bad arrangement, and at the moment seemed to be the only solution to Jack's dilemma, for he was a man of some con-

* The Jack Powell family homesteaded at the eastern end of Ontario's Saganagons Lake.

science and disliked the thought of deserting this girl and his new daughter. In the spring, she wisely persuaded him to quit the woods for the summer and fish with her for their living. This idea proved more profitable than logging, and in the fall, he likewise took her suggestion and became a trapper. She had the ability of her forefathers, and under her able direction the arrangement was again exceedingly profitable. Jack deserted the lumber camp for good. Each year, his common-law wife presented him with a new offspring, which further complicated matters, and in the meantime, he had grown progressively fond of her. Mike was the fourth child, and with the arrival of a son, Jack decided to do something about it. The pair were quietly married in the village and went to live in a luxurious log cabin he had built eighty-six miles to the north on their trapping grounds. At the time of our meeting, the score stood at eleven children, one boy and ten girls. Not one showed the white blood of their father, but for all of that, as I was to learn later, they were a lovely and devoted family.

Mike was fifteen, broad and stocky like his Cornish father. He weighed a hundred and ninety pounds, and I would have guessed his age at twenty-one or better. It fell upon Mike and me to provide meat for both camps, which was no small assignment in the disagreeable weather. He taught me to snare rabbits by placing brush barriers across their almost invisible trails, leaving only a small opening for the game to pass through. A light flexible copper wire, formed into a slip noose and tied firmly to the barrier, circled the runway opening about two inches off the ground. If it failed to close about the rabbit's neck, it invariably tightened just forward of the haunches as he came through, and we then had the makings of a "boo-yah," the French Canadian's version and spelling of bouillon, a semi-thick stew of meat, potatoes, and whatever vegetables are available.

Mike could knock a squirrel off the branch of a tree with a small stone at thirty feet as often as I could by sighting carefully with my rifle, and he picked up several whose curiosity got the better of them as we wandered through the woods. In a nearby thicket, I discovered a pair of spruce hens and shot them for our larder also. They were the first I had ever seen. They are sometimes called fool hens for good reason, and are as tame as chickens, relying on their coloring to protect them. These we baked in clay by wrapping them first in birch leaves, then burying the sticky mass in the coals of our fire. Mike acquainted me with the edible berries of the woods and taught me other valuable Indian lore that served me well on many later occasions.

The fourth day dawned bright and clear, but the rolling breakers forced another day of idleness. Covington lay in front of their tent reading. He was not a particularly sociable chap, and I walked over to try to get better acquainted with him. Here in this primitive environment, I found him reading, of all things, a copy of Darwin's *Descent of Man*. This so aroused my curiosity that I asked him some pointed questions as to his background. At my interrogation, he shut up like a clam and looked on me with apparent disturbed suspicion. When Jack knew me better, he asked what I had said to him back there on the lake and lectured me on wilderness etiquette. It seems that after my inquisitiveness, Covington went to Jack and questioned him carefully and at length as to who I was and what I was doing up there in the woods. There was something peculiar about Archie, and he did not stay long in that area. Jack told me that he was a graduate of the University of Edinburgh and had come to Canada from the British Isles. Beyond that he had been able to learn very little about him, even in their close association, and he admonished me to curb my curiosity with strangers on the back trails. I have often wondered what crime or indiscretion had forced this polished intellectual to take refuge in the comparative security of the woods; surely there was something in back of his furtive anxiety and reticence.

Jack would be home from the patrol in a week, and we accepted a cordial invitation to visit him on our return from the village. The Canadian government had organized the border patrol as a consolidation of three branches of service—fire warden, game warden, and customs agent—and sought out seasoned men for these positions. It did not interfere with Jack's occupation and meant extra money in the summer when he was forced to idleness. He and his wife had discontinued their fishing when they moved to the cabin because the fish could not be kept long enough to get them to market from that distance, and his new job was a welcome replacement of these former activities.

Bill did not say so, but he was anxious to get back to his sweetheart at Four-mile Portage and we paddled hard the next day until early afternoon. We had skipped lunch in the hope of borrowing a cookstove with an oven for a midafternoon meal. I had four partridge and two fat mallards stowed away for this purpose and looked forward with anticipation to a crisp brown stuffed and roasted duck for my dinner.

Frank Chosa's bachelor quarters seemed to be our best bet, and we pulled up at the dock in front of his cabin.* He was at home and hospitably extended us the use of his stove. The birds were already plucked and drawn, and in minutes, bulging with savory dressing, they were sizzling in the oven. We sat in the shade on the porch and absorbed the news of the portage and the village between bastings and replenishing the fire. Frank was a corpse of a man whose only claim to glory was a stretch on a square-rigger in the South Seas and a hitch with Mexican revolutionists below the border. I do not believe I have ever encountered a lazier man. He would wait for days, nearly starving in the meantime, for the right wind to blow him across the bay for supplies, and for the return trip he would wait again, living off his brother, until the wind changed to blow him back. We discovered there was nothing in the house now to eat except some shell macaroni, and in pity invited this derelict to share our meal with us in return for the use of his stove.

The birds looked beautiful in their new golden-brown coats, and the aroma of sage dressing and crisping meat permeated the whole house. Another twenty minutes and they would be done to a turn. Bill and I walked down to the lake to hold our appetites in check and sat on the dock. We saw Frank go into the house but thought nothing of it, and at the end of our twenty minutes, we sauntered back to the cabin. There sat Frank, starting in on the leg of one of the partridge, the bones of two partridge and two mallard already in front

---

* The 1920 census lists Frank Chosa, forty-nine, living with his wife, Caroline, twenty-one, and their three young children in Fall Lake Township, Lake County.

of him. Unembarrassed, he said, "I got so hungry I didn't think you'd care if I started in." I was angry and snatched the leg out of his hand. Bill was as mad as I was, for he was partial to mallard, too, and said, "What in hell d'you think we're gonna eat—macaroni?" Frank knew very well we hadn't eaten, but replied, "Oh! I thought you had already had dinner." Bill and I sat down to what was left in angry silence, finished our meal, and left without even a thank you in either direction. After we had cooled down, we had a good laugh about it, for we realized that it was probably Frank's first decent meal in months, and judging from the stocks in his larder, he was no doubt ravenous.

We set up camp at our old spot on the portage, and on the way over to the store to gather more news of the outside world we dropped in on another friend of Bill's. Vince Burshaw was a dissolute alcoholic who lived like the lilies of the field. His livelihood depended solely on the benevolence of his hardworking Indian wife and the liquid donations of his chance acquaintances. Like a planet, he revolved around his cabin with the shade, in an old cane-bottomed armchair propped against the wall. Inside, his wife worked and soothed his tortured soul with sunny lullabies that came to him through the cheesecloth-covered window as he dozed. I have never heard a more varied vocabulary of epithets and curses than he could muster when the heat of the sun forced him to get out of his chair and move back again into the shade. When it rained, I doubt if he even got out of bed, but I have never been there since to check on it. At least he was a close second to Frank for downright laziness.

At the store, we found that Leo hadn't seen his brother

for a month, but he got a good chuckle from our account of the dinner party. Frank was a constant worry to his brother. Rumor had it that he was selling moon [illegally distilled liquor] to the Indians again. He had been sent up and served time once before on this count, and another charge would go hard with him.

At the town house we found things just as we had left them and spent the day dusting and tidying up the place. We dined on thick beefsteaks that night and went to bed on soft mattresses, but I didn't sleep very well, I guess because there were no hard bough stems, lumpy ground, or rocks to curl around in the mattress. In the morning, we bought our traps and made out two long grocery lists, one to take with us on our return and the other to pick up just before ice closed the canoe routes. The storekeeper had several large orders of semi-perishables like that that must be ready for the north country just before the freeze-up. Trappers would all be in for their final supplies, and even one day's delay might mean frozen lakes that would end canoe travel yet not support a man's weight for as much as two or three weeks of good trapping weather after the freeze.

It started to rain again and kept up a steady drizzle all week. We got out the washtubs and treated our clothes to some honest-to-goodness hot water and real soapsuds, and dried them in our mansion of many rooms. I reveled in the luxury of hot baths in the same tubs, and even dressed up in city clothes for one evening to attend a local dance and social with the sheriff's daughter. The music was colorful if not of modern rhythm. Two Finns sawed feverishly at their fiddles and stamped out the cadence noisily with their heavy boots to the accompaniment of a local damsel at the warped, rusty-stringed piano. It was quite a change for me from our self-imposed isolation in the wild country, but my one night out was enough for me and I was ready to go back to the peace and quiet of our bachelor's retreat.

We left in the rain to keep our appointment with Powell. Basswood Lake kept faith with us again and furnished another experience on our way up. On the north shore, in the late afternoon, we came to an encampment. There was a canoe on the shore, a tent on the bank, and two men and two women standing in front of it. Our curiosity, rather than the discomfort of traveling in the rain, soaked to the skin, held us there for the night to share its misery with these strangers. A certain amount of bad weather was to be expected on the canoe lanes, but company was always a welcome diversion. With the methodical efficiency of long practice, we landed, set up camp, and had a roaring fire going in just about the time it takes to tell it.

Two bedraggled young couples from Chicago watched us with a mixture of admiration, astonishment, and fascination. They stood in front of their drooping tent alongside a weak smudge that the rain was fast reducing to cold ashes as we made ourselves snugly comfortable. While I put up the tent, Bill found an old pine stump. He took the dull blade of the double-bitted ax and cut down below the surface of the ground to some of the old roots that were so saturated with pitch that they were not only waterproofed but quickly inflammable. Some of these he shaved into a torch with his case knife, grubbling out enough additional roots to ensure a quick, hot fire over which to dry out the rain-soaked dead popple we used for cooking. When it is dry, this wood produces a most desirable smokeless fire that will not soot up the utensils. Bill lit a match to the shavings; they burst into flame immediately. Then came the pine roots and the popple.

One of the young women came over to Bill and humbly inquired, "How in the world did you ever start that fire? We have been here four days and have used up all the newspapers and matches in camp, and we haven't had a single fire yet that we could cook on."

Bill explained the use of pitch pine for a sure starter in any weather and invited her and her shivering, disconsolate companions over to warm their numbed bodies as we prepared our evening meal. Their canoe had swamped when they landed, and everything they owned was soaked. In fact, they had slept for three nights in clammy, sodden blankets and had had nothing to eat but unheated canned goods in all that time. We could not help but laugh at four huge packsacks of completely water-soaked store bread, which they had brought with them, that were now reduced to wet, sickly gray, unpalatable mush.

It seemed the proper time for us to play the good Samaritan, so I invited them to have supper with us. They flushed with pleasure at this friendly gesture from strangers and gratefully accepted the invitation. Bill and I chuckled and planned to outdo ourselves in the art of woods cookery. They had a huge, cumbersome coffee pot of about three-gallon capacity—a relic, I gathered, from their church social activities, and coffee which they readily donated toward the meal. We suspended a long green sapling ridgepole between two forked uprights driven into the ground, one on each side of the fire, the fork on one side purposely higher than the other, so that the ridge pole would slant across the flames and allow pots to hang either at a high or low level above the blaze. We cut short forks of green wood about eight inches long and notched the larger prongs of each to take the bails of our kettles. We could then suspend them over the fire at the proper height by hooking the short end of the fork over the ridgepole. Our friends were complete novices and applauded even this simple device.

In no time we had a pot of hot coffee with which we thawed out our guests while the meal was being prepared. Reluctantly, we sacrificed a roast of beef that had been meant as a present for the Powells, cut it up into a large stewing kettle, and started a boo-yah. When the meat was nearly done, adding rice, carrots, onions, turnips, celery, and potatoes, I carefully seasoned the concoction, tasting and testing, watching over the ingredients in the manner of a trained expert. Bill dug a hole in the contents of our flour sack and kneaded some shortening into part of the ingredients. He then added sufficient water to form a ball of dough in the resulting depression. This procedure brought forth an exclamation from one of the girls. She was quite embarrassed, however, when Bill lifted out the mixture, leaving the balance of our flour as dry as ever. Cutting the dough to shape, he placed the biscuits in our baker alongside the fire. As a crowning feat, he also stirred up a bannock and dropped it into our long-handled frying pan in a quarter of an inch of sizzling fat. This woods oddity requires no shortening, is quick to prepare, and if properly made produces a delicious brown pan bread not unlike an English muffin, though lighter, tastier, and more heavily crusted.

The meal was a huge success. Our hungry guests ate more than we did and claimed the stew to be out of this world. Bill says a man has to be hungry to eat my cooking, but at least I had already had the satisfaction of seeing him put twenty pounds on his long lean frame in the short period since we had thrown our lots together. The girls carefully took down the secrets of making bannock to take back to Chicago with them, and Bill and I took our bows, I'm afraid not without some rightful pride in our accomplishments. The neophytes relieved us of the dishes and we dutifully hung up their sodden blankets under a canvas fly and replenished the fire so that not long after dark they crawled into a dry warm comfort in spite of the rain. That night we set our sourdough with buckwheat flour in anticipation of giving them another surprise in the morning.

When we called them for breakfast, their warm smiles were sufficient indication of their acceptance of the invitation, and they gladly furnished coffee for the second time. It seemed about the only salvageable article of food in their entire larder, outside of a few canned goods. Bill had to call a halt on the buckwheat cakes in order to save enough starter for our sourdough pail. Again the girls took down the recipe. With a straight face, Bill explained that the cakes were so light sometimes he had to throw in a little handful of gravel to keep them from floating out of the pan on account of the hot gas bubbles in the frying dough. The girls' puzzled expressions showed that for a moment they had almost accepted Bill's solemn statement as a fact. It was a real pleasure to see these hungry people eat, even though their capacity did put us on short rations for a week.

The sun was out and we prepared to move on. Our friends packed for their return to town, although less than a week of their planned two weeks' vacation had passed. There was nothing else they could do on what remained of their supplies after the mishap. I am not sure whether our chance encounter helped or completely discouraged them; at any rate, their time was too short to make a new start with fresh unwatered stock. We gave them enough matches to see them through and figured that a restricted diet for two days would not materially affect their well-being. These grand people thanked us profusely, exacting our promise of an extended visit if we ever came to Chicago and assuring us they would be back next year properly outfitted for easy luxury living on the waterways of the lake country. Our canoe was loaded in half the time it took them to gather their dunnage together, and we pushed off up the lake as they waved us on our way.

There were two three-quarter-mile portages left to Jack's cabin. The Canadian portages were not as well cut out as those on the border, but once located, they were well packed by many moccasined feet and easy to follow. We arrived in the middle of the afternoon and were met at the canoe dock by the entire baker's dozen: Jack, his wife, and the eleven children, not counting the three ever-present dogs and the two young beaver, pets of the children, one of which swam out to meet us, paddling alongside the canoe as we landed.

Mrs. Powell [Mary Ottertail] was a tall, thin, stoical individual who acknowledged my introduction with a grunt. She was not an old woman, possibly forty, grown old before her time as so many women do with the cares and hardships of constant outdoor toil. The flesh of her lean jaw was plowed into deep, wrinkled furrows that ran from her chin to the characteristic high cheekbones of the full-blooded Chippewa. Jack spoke a few words to her in the Indian language and we filed on up to the cabin.

The house and its furnishings were a complete enigma. Here in this vast expanse of wilderness, nearly a hundred miles from civilization, in a trapper's log cabin, I saw plastered and papered walls; hardwood flooring; a very up-to-date wood range and a circulating heater; mahogany dining room, living room and bedroom suites; and last, but most surprising of all, a beautiful baby grand piano. Jack had bound two canoes together with cross poles to support the heavier pieces, and with the help of his wife and the older children had packed and paddled all of this wealth of sophistication over nine portages and ten lakes from the village to their home.

I have never seen a finer group of children. They all spoke perfect English and bowed or curtsied at our meeting, eager to please and make us welcome to their cabin home, though they were naturally shy and modest before white strangers. Not many outsiders ventured that far back into the wilderness, and outside of Mike, you could count on the fingers of one hand the number of trips the others had made to the village.

Jack's own illiteracy had been the spark that fired his determination to educate his children. He could read and that was about all. Through the superintendent of public schools in the village, to whom he had gone for guidance, he purchased a complete set of grade school manuals. Classes and study were a daily compulsion in his home, except during trapping season. Struggling through the lessons, acting the part of both schoolmaster and student, himself learning as he taught, Jack wrestled with his educational difficulties. There were many problems too difficult for understanding, which he dutifully recorded and took back to the superintendent for explanation. At the time of my visit they were an intelligent group of eighth graders, and I have yet to see a better disciplined one. Their manner of expression was slightly bookish and precise, to be sure, but it was entirely free of modern slang or school-yard vulgarity.

I was most interested in the two bright-eyed little beaver members of this happy family, and learned their history from Mike, the owner. Early in May, Mike had located a large beaver house that lay close in against the shore of one of the lakes. As he passed in his canoe, a large female beaver, heavy with young, lay stretched out on the roof of her abode, sunning herself. From then on, he watched her closely. In the matter of a few days she no longer appeared for her sunbaths and Mike correctly surmised the young had arrived. He waited until he was sure the little ones would have their eyes open and be up and about, exploring their new world. Paddling down the lake, he pushed his canoe into the grass a hundred yards below the house, made a wide detour, and cautiously approached on moccasined feet from the land side. With three last swift strides, he leaped upon the huge mound of moss and mud-thatched cuttings, landing with all the force he could muster, at the same time letting out a blood-curdling whoop that startled the occupants within. The mother, apparently, dove through the subterranean entrance for open water without collecting her wits or leaving instructions for the newborn young. Two of the little fellows instinctively followed her, but as they had not yet been taught to dive, they were unable to submerge after coming to the surface for air. Mike swam out and captured them before they could seek cover, and he and the family had raised them on a bottle, with condensed milk, until they were now as tame as kittens.

Beaver have four principal teeth, which are the tools they use in their natural environment for felling the trees with which they build their houses and dams; the succulent bark of these same trees also provides them with the main part of their winter diet. The two lower incisors act as a brace against which the upper ones are drawn down through the wood, much in the same manner as a carpenter would use a grooving chisel. The upper teeth are curved slightly inwards. They are very sharp, and even in these little fellows they were already over an inch long. I have seen old cuttings where trees a foot and a half in diameter have been felled by these busy little engineers.

The most desirable tree is the popple, whose green, tender, easy-to-peel bark is their favorite food. When they are very hungry, they will also eat the bark of alder and white birch, but cuttings of these woods are used primarily in building. Popple waterlogs quickly, and beaver are quick to take advantage of this fact. Late in the fall you will find a huge stockpile of short branches completely submerged in deep water in front of the house, well below the freezing line. To start the pile, the beaver weight a few small branches to the bottom with stones or mud and then progressively tuck in underneath the anchor pile, from all sides, larger branches in jackstraw confusion, until they have a sufficient quantity of bark to last through the winter, right at their door.

At suppertime, I found the answer for one of the queerest sights I had ever seen and one that I had pondered from the time of my arrival. Every piece of the Powells' beautiful furniture that stood on legs had the legs wrapped in tin from the sides of gallon fruit cans, parts of the labels still on them, wired in place with common stovepipe wire. Underneath the tin on one leg of the bed were long, ugly gouges where one of the beaver, carelessly left alone for a moment, had practiced his powers as a woodsman and sharpened his teeth in the soft mahogany.

As we sat down, one of the younger girls pulled up an extra chair and brought in one of the pet beaver. The little fellow sat up to the table as straight as a drum major, his bright intelligent eyes watching our every move. His long claws clung to the edge of the table as he surveyed the food and waited to be served. Mrs. Powell had purposely mashed potatoes for the performance and when we were all served, the beaver was given a fork and a dish of mashed potatoes also. He speculatively watched us eat and managed to load his fork in a passable Emily Post style, but when it came to getting the food into his mouth, his troubles began. The big teeth almost blocked the opening, and he smeared more potato in his whiskers than he was able to get past these barriers. They gave him an aluminum measuring cup of canned milk which he picked up by the handle in perfect mimicry of our example, but again the two long incisors in the front of his upper jaw got in the way. It was necessary for him to get these inside the cup first, and when this was accomplished, the lower teeth held the cup away from his lips far enough so that, when he drank, as much milk dribbled down the front of his soft pearly waistcoat of fur as reached his throat.*

Our laughter seemed to be an acknowledgment of our approval of his performance, and he actually looked pleased with himself at our applause. When the assembly ignored him completely, he reverted to type, set down his implements, and dove into the mashed potatoes with both paws, easily circumventing his teeth by pushing the food in from each side. It was an act surpassing that of any vaudeville headliner whose performance I had ever witnessed.

Beaver are great imitators and attempt any task they see performed. Mrs. Powell carried in firewood from a neatly corded pile some twenty feet from the cabin. She deposited her supply in the corner of the kitchen next to the stove with a supporting cross pile at the end to keep it in order. When the flies were not bad, she could leave the screen door open, start the pile, and the beaver would do the rest, working like little Trojans, cross piling the end as square and true as though guided by a carpenter's plumb line. When they tired of their work, they would lie on their fat bellies wherever they happened to be and sleep for possibly fifteen minutes, then get up and go at it again with renewed vigor. They were industrious little creatures and seemed to sense the necessity of keeping a supply of wood on hand against the rainy day.

Jack's family had another unbelievable accomplishment.

* This story and the one that follows are probably tall tales.

Each member played some form of musical instrument, and they proudly brought out and displayed their shiny treasures to us. There were two violins, two saxophones, a cornet, trombone, banjo, piccolo, guitar, snare drum, and the piano. That night, Jack the maestro led his little orchestra through a repertoire of folk songs, hymns, and martial music that boomed along the low rafters of the cabin and caused the dishes to dance excitedly on the kitchen shelves.

As was to be expected, all of them were star marksmen, and they possessed high-caliber rifles of bore and mechanism conforming to their individual tastes and performance appraisals. Heavily greased and in their individual cases, the rifles stood in a gun rack along a wall of the dining room, which looked like the arsenal of a national guard unit. These experts were a definite menace to any of the larger animals and marauders of the forest and, should the occasion arise, they would without question have presented a formidable company of sharpshooters.

During the trapping season, the family split up into pairs. One older person always stayed at home with the two youngest children and set traps and snares in the vicinity of the cabin; the others picked their favorite companion and in groups of two struck out on snowshoes, packs on their backs, for thirty-day periods on their assigned trapping grounds. There was a great deal of rivalry to see who could bring in the most fur, and the crowning glory was to beat their father, who teamed up with his favorite, Mike. Jack supervised the crews and placed the more ambitious and experienced pairs in the territories where the highest-priced fur was to be found. Fisher, martin, otter, mink, and silver fox were the most sought after animals, and the most difficult to outwit. Mrs. Powell and her oldest daughter were the stiffest competition, and more often than not, they brought in the prize catches. Beaver were plentiful, were easy to trap, and brought good prices on the market. The young folks concentrated on these animals, although all teams watched for dams, houses, and cuttings, and never missed an opportunity to swell their take with extra beaver pelts.

Jack had over a hundred of the most beautiful, carefully selected, fully prime, matched muskrat hides that one could imagine. They had been willow-tanned in Indian fashion by Mrs. Powell and the girls, and were as soft as a chamois. I made a dicker for them there and then, and bought the lot. To make change, Jack walked me out to his cash register, about forty yards from the house. To my surprise, he kicked over a small boulder and exposed a tin box with over six thousand dollars in it. He did not believe in banks, and casually informed me that the family had over forty thousand dollars in similar caches conveniently placed around the cabin. After expenses were taken care of, all members of the family received equal shares of the profits to do with as they saw fit. The box I had been taken to was the family exchequer, from which all collective expenses were paid. I asked Jack how he dared take such chances and show a relative stranger his hiding place, suggesting that I might return in the night and steal his money.

He grinned and replied laconically, "You wouldn't get very far," and I am inclined to believe that his statement was correct. He would have been a relentless pursuer.

I could see now how they could afford all the home luxuries of the better classes in the city. We stayed four days, at Jack's insistence, with this unusual family, and I felt grieved to think of what the fates had decreed for such pleasant, capable, and intelligent children.

It was high time we paid attention to our own preparations and set off for home. The next two weeks were spent in splitting cedar shakes and shaping them into stretchers to receive our prospective catch. This was counting live pelts while they still ran free in the forest, but we were confident of at least some degree of success, and there would be no time to count them later when the fur was prime. Daily we saw mink, muskrat, and beaver right from our headquarters windows. There were boards shaped for weasel, muskrat, mink, otter, fox, fisher, and even wolves, and we tied bows of alder by the dozen on which to sew and stretch our beaver pelts. Everything was in readiness to receive the catch.

At this point it seemed advisable to make a quick trip to town and bring back our season's supply of onions, potatoes, beets, carrots, parsnips, rutabagas, winter apples, dried apricots, peaches, pears, prunes, and two cases of fresh eggs. The eggs we put down in water glass,* the beets, carrots, and parsnips were planted in fresh moist beach sand, the rutabagas were dipped in hot paraffin, and all were stored in our cold, frost-proof rock vault beneath the cabin. The preparations gave us a comfortable, satisfying feeling of self-sufficiency, and we waited for the freeze-up, secure in the thought that one trip over the ice for sugar and flour would complete our stores for the long winter ahead.

* Water glass is a sodium-silicate compound, soluble in water and alcohol, that was used to preserve eggs.

Prospecting our territory was good preliminary training to put us in shape for the daily grind of a trapline, and I enjoyed the long cross-country hikes that took us through timber, over open hills, along the lakeshores, into tangled slashings and burnt-over country, and around dense swamps. All we carried was our guns and a light lunch, a weight that reduced our labors to a minimum. We kept a sharp lookout for game but did very little shooting. With meat so plentiful, it was like going to the butcher shop; if the quality did not suit us, or we were too far from camp, we waited another day. In our market, however, the price was always right; the cost a single bullet, for we made sure of our marks. Sooner or later we would find a fat yearling buck or moose practically on our doorstep, for we saw them almost every day on our excursions.

The country to the east was very rugged, and the day we explored this region Bill and I both carried our rifles. There were rocky ridges of slate and low-grade iron ore, separated by deep valleys down which rushing streams tumbled and boiled over the rocks. Topping the rise of one mountain of iron after a stiff climb, we stopped to catch our breath before making the descent and almost missed seeing two large timber wolves that we had apparently surprised as they drank from the stream. They had seen us first and were frozen into motionless gray statues that blended perfectly with the barren hillside. When I discovered them, I threw up my rifle and yelled to Bill, "Take the left one." Then the bombardment began. My first bullet ricocheted off the rocks and sailed humming over the hill like a hornet. All of our shots were going wild, throwing up dust on all sides of the fleeing animals and whining viciously off into the distance. The wolves were stretched out like whippets at the track in their wild scramble up the ridge. I missed time and time again, and Bill was doing no better. I was down to two bullets and knew that in my eagerness I had been firing too rapidly. I calmed down for the next shot and aimed carefully. Wham! Over he went, end over end, like a stick of cordwood. Bill had steadied down also, and had the same good fortune. We had two fair pelts to bring in and a soft bushy tail apiece with which to line our winter parka hoods. In addition to this there was a thirty-dollar bounty for us to anticipate.

The weather was turning colder and there were crystal-clear ice splinters hanging on the marsh grasses along the lakeshores that sparkled and tinkled in the early-morning breeze like tiny sleigh bells. The deer mice, searching for winter quarters, came into our cabin in droves. We had anticipated their arrival and had provided ourselves with two large steel lard drums for storing our packages of cereals and flour. There they stood in the corner, empty. Before we were aware of their presence, the mice had torn the sacks and packages to shreds. While our loss was not great, we paid for our tardiness and spent half a day cleaning up the mess.

When the temperature snapped down in earnest, we had a nocturnal visitor that put an end to these depredations in a hurry. We first noticed him just about sundown peeking out from the water well underneath our foot-powered grindstone, his two beady, phosphorescent eyes glowing inquiringly in the dusk as we prepared our evening meal. He made his home under our woodpile, but came into our shack to do his hunting. We were often awakened from a sound sleep by a frantically squeaking mouse scurrying along the rafter poles and wall beams, the weasel in hot pursuit. Suddenly the commotion would cease and deathly silence ensued as the little marauder trotted off with his prey for the feast. Our visitor grew bolder as time went on, and one night as we lay in our bunks listening to a particularly lively chase, the squeaking quarry crossed and recrossed the rafters. You could hear both the pursued and the pursuer clawing desperately for a foothold on the smooth poles as they raced along. Directly over my bed—I will never know whether he slipped and fell or jumped in terror—the mouse came hurtling down to land directly on my stomach. Undaunted, the weasel followed, hitting the exact spot from which the mouse a split second before had scrambled hastily to the floor. Our mouse troubles ended here, for I believe this one was the last victim of our benefactor.

We took to feeding the weasel at mealtimes, and coming from the trail we often held a partridge head down over the grindstone well from where the little glutton watched for us to come home. With surprising agility he would pop out of the well, hook his needle-sharp eyeteeth behind the skull of the bird, and instantly decapitate him, laying bare the tender brains, which he scooped out avariciously in one operation. During a heavy cold spell, when the temperature dropped to a mere fifty below, a wild yell from Bill untwisted me from a cozy ball into which I wound myself in the night. "Light the light! Light the light!" he shouted. Fully aroused, I jumped out of bed and put a match to the kerosene lamp, wondering what sort of nightmare had so ruffled Bill's usual composure. I peered into the shadows and there, sitting upright in bed, was Bill, with a stranglehold on the weasel's neck, the animal kicking his last between Bill's strong fingers. Bill had awakened in the night to find the bloodthirsty little rascal firmly attached to the lobe of his ear, drinking his fill. That ended our house pets.

An old beaver, probably an outcast from one of the nearby houses, took up bachelor's quarters under our boathouse and was busily engaged in hauling in fresh-cut popple beneath the dock for his winter food. We watched his ceaseless efforts and ruthlessly thought that he would be a handy guinea pig to trap for testing the primeness of fur when the weather turned colder. The restless activity of all the furbearers and the great flocks of ducks and geese that passed over daily were mute evidence that we would soon be rousing from our carefree lethargy and hard at work ourselves.

In the night, without warning, the temperature dove to twenty below and there was a quarter of an inch of flint-hard ice on the narrows, but we were still confident that the sun would dissipate this early cold wave. The next night, twenty-eight below was recorded and we tested the ice by walking across to the point opposite our cabin. There was still a large pool of open water below the dam. As we watched, a mink struggled to the surface of the water at the edge of the ice that surrounded the pool. He backed onto the smooth surface as though he carried a great weight in his mouth. For several moments he tugged and hauled, gaining a little advantage, then losing it on the slippery ice. Finally, to our complete amazement, he dragged out a northern pike fully twice his own length and three times his weight, and proceeded to dine on his catch. I can only surmise that, in some manner, this little fellow with his awl-like teeth had struck a telling blow at some nerve center, rendering his quarry hapless before he brought him to the surface.

WINTER WAS HERE, and we were caught wholly unprepared in many departments. We got out our seine and tried to figure a way to stretch it across the mouth of the still-unfrozen river below the falls by canoe, but ended up waist deep in the bone-chilling eddies harvesting our winter's supply of whitefish. These fish had likewise not anticipated an early freeze, for they had just started to run. Spawning in the fall, they gather in great schools below the obstructions that block their passage upstream. We were fortunate that three attempts rewarded our efforts with eight hundred pounds of these silver beauties, for it was about all we could stand, and we were glad to get back to the warm cabin and dry clothing. We cleaned, scaled, and packed in salt three hundred pounds, hastily set up smoking racks and smoked another two hundred pounds, and piled the other three hundred pounds like cordwood on the shady side of our cabin to freeze for the winter.

The ice was strong enough now to carry our weight, and we brought in the balance of our supplies from the village by toboggan. On our way home, it was Bill's turn at pulling the toboggan and I was walking about thirty yards ahead on the lake's smooth surface. The wind was sharp and raw, and I headed for the lee of a small island near the farther shore of the lake, slowed up in its shelter, and waited for Bill to catch up.

Around the point, on the glaring ice and twenty yards from shore, a small doe sat on her haunches and busily struck with her knife-sharp forefeet at two attacking wolves, who lunged at her throat in a crisscross manner, first one from one side and the other following quickly from the opposite side, back and forth, back and forth; they were giving the animal no rest. They had driven the doe on purpose onto the slippery ice, where the poor creature could not hold her feet nor move swiftly in defense, and had then cut the cords on her hind legs, hamstringing her with their razor-sharp teeth just below the haunches. Her hind legs were now useless. We watched for a breathless minute as she struck out bravely at her attackers, but finally their opportunity came. One of the doe's feet slipped on the glossy surface and she was unable to ward off the blow. A leaping wolf, who in previous lunges had treated her hoofs with due respect, shot out his long lean neck and clamped his teeth in her throat. They came away with a large portion of fur, flesh, and windpipe tightly clasped in the powerful jaws, torn out by the sheer weight of the wolf's heavy, swinging body as it completed its arc. He rolled over and over from his fall, but recovered himself and returned for the feast as the hot blood spurted from the gaping hole in the doe's neck. She sank down slowly in the quickly spreading pool of her own lifeblood. We had no guns, but intervened at this point, robbing the wolves of their kill. When they saw us, they hastily ran for shore and disappeared in the bushes.

I waited a week, like a high-strung thoroughbred at the

starting gate, but Bill displayed no enthusiasm and scoffed derisively at my suggestion that fur must be prime now with all the cold weather we had been having. Killing time with my shotgun, I picked up seventy-five black mallards from a flock that passed over the dam twice daily. There were about three hundred of them that apparently planned to stay the winter in the small openings below the dam and falls of the vicinity, where the open water made snails and other food available. I froze fifty partridge and brought in a nice fat yearling buck.

Such beautiful days: crisp, heady morning air that gave you the feeling of having taken a stimulant each time you filled your lungs, sunshine that sparkled on the white fluffy snow and warmed you into lazy afternoon drowsiness. With my rifle on my shoulder, I crisscrossed the country scouting new signs of furbearers and planning my traplines.

On one of these days, when the temperature stood at around fourteen degrees below zero, I came upon one of the strangest sights I had ever witnessed. The countryside was a solid blanket of white, but ahead of me I could see one black splotch about thirty feet across. It wasn't bare ground, I was sure. I walked up to the spot and couldn't believe my eyes. There, in sub-zero weather, were millions of tiny black flies with iridescent gossamer wings, resting on the snow. They had the same shape and appearance as the sand fly or Green Bay fly, so common around the streetlights and store windows in summer. I had heard of snow flies, but put it down as a wilderness myth dreamed up by some snow-blind traveler. Where they come from, and how they hatch and survive sub-zero weather, is still a mystery to me. When I disturbed them, they took off in a swarm and disappeared over the hill.

On one of my wanderings, I discovered a beaver dam that someone apparently had dynamited. It was a small creek, and I could picture the helpless animals seeking cover as the pond drained of water. Apparently the marauders had killed off all of the inhabitants, as there had been no attempt at repairing the damage and all the cuttings were old ones, made early in the fall. As I stood there on the ridge to which the dam had been attached, I was conscious of a strong light striking me in the eyes, as though someone flashed a large mirror in the sun, deflecting the light into my face. Following the direction from which it came, I couldn't see anything, and yet from time to time the flash appeared and went off like the semaphore communication lights on a battleship.

It must have been close to two miles away, but my curiosity got the better of me and I trudged on over. There was a long ridge slowly ascending out of the valley ahead of me in a direct line with where I had seen the flashes, and I decided it would be a good vantage point from which to observe my phenomena. As I proceeded up the ridge, I could see that it ended at the edge of about forty acres of sparsely covered alder swamp. The last thirty yards of the ridge rose abruptly into a high rocky promontory, and I reached the summit slowly and completely out of breath. Right below me, not twenty yards away, feeding in a clump of alders, stood a big cow moose. I flattened myself immediately and lay on my stomach as still as a corpse. There was another very bright flash, this time on the farther side of the marsh about two hundred yards away, and I made out the outline of a huge bull partially concealed in the brush. His spread of antlers was enormous, eight feet, I judged, at the least. I had never seen any that would equal them in any lodge or city club I had ever visited. I wanted that trophy, though Lord only knows what for, or where I would put it if I were fortunate enough to bring him down.

I looked the marsh over carefully and counted nine more bulls, all of considerable size, feeding peaceably in the thickets, but none that would equal the big fellow opposite me. He raised his head once more, reaching for a morsel of tender twigs above him, and again the reflection of the sun on the highly polished surface of the broad hand of his horn blinded me temporarily. The cow below me was getting nervous. I was downwind from the herd, but she sensed that something was wrong. She had stopped eating and let out several nervous snorts and pawed the frozen ground. At the warning the entire herd raised their heads, listening and sniffing the wind. The cow looked in all directions and then moved slowly away from me. The rest of the herd, with the exception of the big bull, also moved slowly toward the timber. I had my rifle trained on him but knew that he would have to break out of the brush before I could get in a telling shot. There must have been a stray current of air that suddenly brought my scent directly to the cow; she instantly snorted again and broke into a fast, comical, stiff-legged trot across the marsh. My prize was the first of the bulls to break into a run, but they all started for the timber almost simultaneously. When I could determine the direction he was taking, I held on the first clear opening he would cross, and as his huge form came into my sights, I fired. The report reverberated back and forth between the hills and sent the herd crashing for the timber in panic. I didn't get a second chance, and in no time the entire herd was out of sight.

With considerable misgiving, I crossed the marsh and took up the trail. A few feet beyond the point where I fired at him, I discovered dark red patches on the snow and my hopes soared. He was hit, and from the color of the blood, I was bold enough to presume that it was a fatal shot in some part of his arterial system. Some thirty yards inside the timber, I found him. My bullet had almost missed; too high for the heart, it had cut between the ribs and gone completely through the flesh just under the backbone, cutting the large artery that follows the vertebrae the full length of the skeleton.

I couldn't believe his size. He must have weighed in the neighborhood of a ton, and I couldn't begin to turn him over. It looked like I had an impossible job on my hands. With my case knife, I cut the hide from well back of the shoulders down to the lower point of the brisket and skinned it back from the neck itself, so that I could get at the underside and slit the hide there also. The head was now free from the carcass. It must have weighed several hundred pounds. I had great difficulty in turning my trophy over, but finally got it resting on the nose and the horns, where I skinned out the neck, cutting it off at the base of the skull and relieving me of this useless excess weight. Just the head and horns I estimated at around two hundred pounds, and it gave me a tussle when I raised it onto two saplings that I cut and left hanging to their stumps to support the head and keep it off the ground, where it would dry out without rotting the hide. It was now late afternoon and I still had ten miles to go to reach camp. I quickly dressed out the carcass and dragged the offal away from the meat, but had to leave the huge frame lying on its side right where it fell.

Bill had gone to town and left me a note telling me of his whereabouts. It was up to me to return in the morning with a toboggan and bring in what I could. I was more concerned with my prize antlers than I was with the meat, but dutifully skinned out the loins and hams and tied them to the toboggan. It was a full day's job getting the meat back to camp, and I knew I had a bigger one facing me in the morning. If Bill had been there, it wouldn't have been such a struggle. If I laid the head flat on the toboggan, the horns stuck out and tangled in the brush; if I put the horns down, the head stuck in the air and my load was top-heavy. The best plan seemed to be to center the head crossways, horns in the air lengthwise, with two six-inch-diameter saplings on the outer edges to brace it in position. It was all I could do to start the load, and the grades were really tough. The least side pitch to the ground and the load skidded off at right angles. I would then have to roll toboggan, head and all, over and over, back onto the crest of the rise. Four o'clock came, and I was still five miles from camp—with rough up and down terrain ahead of me. I found a big pine stump and decided to plant my treasure on it until I could return with help. It was all I could handle, but skidding and rolling it up the smooth bottom of the toboggan, I got it in place and went on in. It snowed twelve inches that night, and I knew I would have to wait for the sun to pack down the snow before finishing my project. We were now well supplied with meat for all winter.

Bill still insisted it was too early to trap. With all his superior woods knowledge, I began to suspect that I was experiencing some of the bullheadedness that Leo warned me about, and secretly I made a set for a muskrat on a close-by marsh. My efforts were rewarded the next morning, and I brought in a pelt that was heavily furred and fully prime. Bill was furious and sulked for four days. I could stand it no longer and told Bill that we would either start trapping in the morning, or I would split the territory with him and go it alone. He made no move to get ready and was sullen and disagreeable the balance of the day.

We had two townships registered in our names. I asked him which he wanted and obtained a grunt for an answer. I offered to split our territory in any direction he wished, but made no headway. Suddenly I remembered the old beaver under the boathouse. Maybe additional proof would bring Bill around. I set a trap for the old bachelor while Bill was out picking cranberries, and had him fast in the morning when I went out to investigate. The grizzly old fellow was just as prime as the muskrat except for two or three tiny pin-points of blue on the hide, just back of the skull, which I laid to old age. Usually unprime skins have blue patches of hide just back of the forelegs. Bill nearly blew a fuse and ranted and raved over the blue specks, swearing the hide would only bring us half price. This was enough for me, and I asked, "Since when do you have jurisdiction over my actions or any claim to the beaver hide? I told you we would either start trapping together, split the territory and go it alone, or I would pay no attention to boundaries and go it alone any-way, and that's what I'm doing." He calmed down for a moment, and I reiterated my offer to make a fair division of the territory in any direction he wished. I mentioned the fact that we had a good summer together and that it was a shame to split up in this manner over petty grievances, but he again crawled into his shell and we never mentioned it again. We ate together regularly, and I tried to be cheerful and went out of my way to do more than my share; at the same time, I was preparing to start in in earnest as soon as I could get my duffel together. Bill sat around and sulked.

Two days later, I took off for the upper shack, feeling that as it was just a stopover, Bill would take his choice of the other two while I was gone, and we could then set up permanent separate quarters. I surveyed the territory, built cubbies to keep snow off my permanent sets, made open water sets for beaver, mink, and muskrat, and put out bait where later I would make sets for fox and wolf.

On trips that held me close to camp, I carried my gun; there was always the possibility of picking up an extra pelt along the way. Cutting across country one day to a long lake on my route, reckoning by the sun, I hit it about at its middle, coming out on a high embankment. At the far end, there was an island; the balance of the lake was a clear expanse of snow-covered ice. Just below me, about at the middle, sat a beautiful silver black fox, not over two hundred yards away. His rich winter coat glistened in the sun and I could see the immaculate white silver tip on his unusually bushy tail. He was totally unaware of my presence, and I was well concealed by the low bushes. I leaned against a tree and took careful aim with my rifle. That pelt would be a prize and I wanted it badly.

At the report of the gun, the snow spurted into the air just over the fox's back. I had missed. The confused fox looked anxiously around, trying to locate the impending danger, and then sped straight up the lake for the island. He could have made the brush of the opposite shore in one-fourth the time, but apparently he had decided that speed and distance were more to his advantage. My next shot threw up a puff of snow just in front of him, the third hit just behind him, and the fourth went under his belly between his flying front and rear legs. Each report urged him on to greater speed, and he was traveling like a comet, his body extended along the ice, tail out straight behind him. I put in two more wild shots for luck, but woefully watched him disappear onto the island. He had won a good race, but was visibly tired from his eight-hundred-yard dash and slowed to a trot as he reached cover.

It was a busy week. My luck was phenomenal and I worked late into the nights skinning and stretching my fur. Our separation perturbed me, and I decided on a quick run down to headquarters to try to bring about a reconciliation with my partner. I packed my wealth of fur, made my trapline, and late in the day started off. It was nine o'clock when I got in. Bill was gone. His outfit was spread out in the usual places, and I figured he must have planned to stay there, so I prepared to establish my headquarters at the O'Niel cabin. My traps were the important thing, and I packed a heavy load for the stopover shack since I would now be spending a large part of my time there. I left my pelts in a conspicuous spot so that Bill could not miss seeing their prime condition and returned early the next morning to my camp.

The next week I came down light. There was no indication that Bill had returned, and with some misgivings I packed a load of supplies on the toboggan for the O'Niel shack. If Bill was there, I would at least save him the trouble of bringing the stuff over. When I arrived, I found that this shack had not been occupied either. My conclusion was that Bill had gone to town for another partner, and I proceeded to set up housekeeping at the O'Niel residence. At daylight the next morning, I cut cross-country, picking up one end of my trapline on the way in.

During the next two weeks, I consolidated my traps with the idea of using the O'Niel shack for headquarters and the stopover for one-night stands as it had been planned for. The weather was perfect, cold nights and warm days, and I worked feverishly to lean up areas that I would soon abandon as too far from my new headquarters. I rather expected Bill to get curious and pay me a visit, but he never showed up.

I picked up the traps on the far end of my run and reset part of them on the way over to the O'Niel shack, where I could watch them to greater advantage. Bill had not been there. In the morning, I threw out another string of traps to the south and east, and tried to cross a big lake below the shack on the young ice to get at a large beaver house where I had seen what I thought to be a family of fine black beaver.

The ice didn't look too good and with ominous ripping noises sent out jagged little iridescent cracks in the clear surface from each spot where I set a foot down heavily to test it. I decided to try it, however, with precautions, and cut two twenty-foot dry tamarack poles to carry with me, one in each hand. There was no snow on this spring-fed lake, as it was very deep and had frozen over only recently, but I put on snowshoes to spread my weight over a larger area of ice and, pack on my back, slithered along with rhythmic continuous motion—not daring to hesitate for a moment, my poles parallel to the ice at the end of my stiffened arms so that, if I did break through, I would not immerse beyond possibly my hips in the paralyzingly cold water. It was twenty-eight below zero. The ice bowed beneath me and came back again as I passed, only to bow again at each new position. Had I been able to turn around, I would have done so, for the ice was getting thinner by the second and continuous motion was my only salvation. I held my breath as I passed the middle of the lake and breathed easier as the further shore came closer, and then—down I went, with a tinkling crash, like the sound of a heavy plate-glass window suddenly shattered and falling on a cement sidewalk.

The poles bisected the hole I had made and there I hung, hip-deep in water like a gymnast on parallel bars. The ice held on both sides of the hole and I inched to the side and forward, getting a greater surface of ice for my poles to rest on. I tried repeatedly to throw myself forward on the ice, my two poles beneath me, but each time a snowshoe hooked under either the poles or the ice, and I was unable to extricate myself. Finally I got my pack off and slid it shoreword on the ice with as much force as I could muster in my hampered position and struggled frantically underwater with the lacings of my right snowshoe. At last it came loose and I slid it ahead on the ice also. My other snowshoe I left on and got that leg onto the ice, then threw myself forward on my poles, inching along anxiously. The ice held beneath them, and I moved first one pole and then the other forward—inches at a time—

until I was several yards beyond the hole. Here it seemed safe to raise up on my arms, dragging my body between the poles, using them like a pair of skis attached to my hands. I slid them along on the smooth surface until I reached my pack and the other snowshoe. The ice seemed heavier here and I gingerly got back onto my feet. The surface cracked in all directions with loud, groaning noises that protested my weight, but it held and I hotfooted it swiftly for shore. It was a harrowing experience and one that could easily have ended disastrously for me.

There was no question of setting traps now. My fingers were frostbitten and my heavy stag pants* had frozen solid around my numb and all but lifeless legs. I cached my traps and set off rapidly for the shack, this time around the end of the lake. The exertion started my blood to circulating again, and I thawed out my hands underneath my jumper. My frozen pants cut my knees at every step, and I could see the brittle frozen fibers breaking at each bend of the material. By the time I reached the shack, they had nearly broken off and the legs hung on by only a few shreds. I thought my teeth would splinter, they chattered so loudly. I started a quick fire with dry cedar and some of our precious illuminating kerosene, and it was two hours before I completely thawed out and got back to normal. The balance of the day I spent in putting in additional cubbies and getting things in shape for efficient timesaving operation. That night, I skinned out pelts until two o'clock in the morning.

Half the day was gone before I crawled out of bed and, af-

---

* Work pants cut off short to dry quickly and avoid dangerous cuffs that could trip the wearer.

ter a hurried breakfast, headed for our original headquarters, which I now called Bill's shack. He had been there recently, but things were hardly disturbed. Apparently he had only stayed one night. His traps were still in the corner. I divided the food as fairly as I could and stacked my share in a pile ready to be transported to O'Niel's cabin as fast as I could spare the time, setting aside a heavy load to take with me in the morning.

Back at the O'Niel shack, I stocked the root cellar with the perishables, made one trapline before dark, ate supper, and went to bed, exhausted. My traps were sadly neglected, but in spite of that, I was taking more fur than I could handle. In the morning, I finished the lines around the cabin, left the frozen animals in the shack to be skinned out later, and pushed on for the stopover, arriving just after dark with another heavy load of fur.

I spent two days here, skinning out my catch and putting the camp in good shape. There was one innovation here, the product of my inventive mind, that I was proud of. The "Chic Sale"* was a drafty affair of cedar poles set close together, its one modern requisite a planed and sanded two-holer seat, each aperture carved individually to accommodate the slim and the broad of beam. There were covers to match, with screw hooks on the underside from which to suspend our storm lantern. In the morning, one could rush out fully clothed, hook the lantern into position under the cover, drop it into the hole, and go back in for breakfast. In fifty-below weather, you can imagine the comfort a well-warmed seat

* A euphemism for privy. Charles ("Chic") Sale wrote *The Specialist*, a humorous best-seller about a man who built outhouses.

afforded when, after breakfast, it became necessary to bare yourself to the elements. One more trip to Bill's camp, and I could eliminate from my worries the necessity of returning there. I had pelts all over the place, which I decided to take in with me. A final inspection of the trapline put everything in good condition. I hadn't seen Bill for a month and was curious to know what had taken place. Besides, there were a few odds and ends to pick up to complete my move.

When I arrived at his camp the next day, there he sat, tipped back in an old wicker chair we had salvaged and repaired with willow twigs, calmly drawing on an old corncob pipe. I greeted him cordially and received an answering grunt, unloaded the toboggan and fluffed up my bunk and bedroll and started supper. Finally Bill spoke: "Movin' out, hey?" I explained that as his duffel was all still there, I assumed he wanted this shack for his own, and that I moved to the O'Niel shack and established my headquarters there. I told him I had been living most of the time at the stopover, but needed a place where I had facilities for baking and keeping things from freezing. He made no reply. When I called him for supper, he moved to the table and put away an enormous meal with seeming enjoyment. I decided to stay over and waste a valuable day in an attempt to settle our differences. I cooked the things Bill liked and made repeated attempts at conversation, but when the silence became embarrassing, I decided it was hopeless and prepared to pull out.

As I was leaving in the morning, he finally opened up and said, "We'll both use all three shacks."

"Okay," I replied, and started off with my load. This looked as though he might be unbending and that we would again be working together in peace and friendship. I hurried on to the O'Niel shack and deposited my load. All of my accessories for comfortable living were now in the one place, and I could give my undivided attention to the trapline.

One thing I did need was flour. Now was the best time to get it, as O'Niel's shack was the closest point to town. The morning stars were still blinking down at me as I stepped onto the lake. The crisp, cold air was invigorating, and I crunched happily along on my snowshoes, the empty toboggan hissing over the snow behind me. On the big lake, I came across the remains of a deer, and then another one. They had, no doubt, been pulled down and devoured by a roving wolf pack. All that remained were a few patches of hide and three lower leg bones, partially blown over with drifting snow. I had seen so much evidence of their nightly slaughtering that I hardly hesitated.

At two o'clock I entered the general store and post office, bought my flour and all the luxuries I could think of, including fresh meat for supper and a ten-pound roast of beef to take back, picked up the mail, and retired to the town house. In our absence, someone had broken in.

A flashlight and a twenty-five-caliber automatic were missing. Further investigation showed that the prowler had also taken a quantity of preserves and canned goods from the basement and several articles of clothing. I built up the fires and took a hot bath before supper. As I stood naked in the washtub, there was a knock on the door and I yelled, "Come in." One of the neighbor boys, whom I had befriended, stepped in self-consciously and asked if I had any work for him. He had split wood and done other chores for us in the past. I told him I was just there for the night and there was nothing I needed, but he hung around as though he had something to tell me, and didn't know just how to begin. I finished my bath and encouraged him with some chocolates I had received from home. Finally he asked, "Did you sell your automatic?"

I replied, "No, but someone has broken into the house and it has been stolen, along with a lot of other valuable things. I will call the sheriff as soon as I'm dressed."

"I know who done it," he offered.

"Who?" I asked.

"You won't tell I told you, will ya?" he inquired.

"Of course not," I replied. He then gave me an account of seeing the boys breaking in and carrying away the stuff. He was a good boy and had wanted to repay me for my kindness to him.

I went straight to the house of the one I knew to be the leader, called him and his mother together, and told him before her just how he entered and mentioned the flashlight, gun, and food. "If you have everything back inside of an hour, I won't say anything, but if you miss a single item, I shall call the sheriff and have you and Marty both arrested and put in jail." This was the first time I had mentioned his accomplice, and before he could recover from his surprise, I turned and slammed the door as I went out.

Just under an hour later, he appeared at the door with his mother. She was crying and explained that they had eaten two jars of the jam. "Bring the stuff in," I replied sternly. Everything I had found missing was there, plus a new rain-proof jacket that I had not noticed was gone. I made a pretense of checking it, had the boy put it away where he had found it, and, at his mother's pleading, agreed to forget the jam. I gave her a good talking to on accepting stolen goods and starting her boy on a life of crime, and told them to leave.

The storekeeper told me the father was a drunkard and the family destitute. He had gone as far as he could and had a big unpaid bill on his books at the present time. I arranged for him to give them a week's further credit before cutting them off, and suggested he garnishee the father's paycheck. At least the money would then go for food instead of whiskey.

That night, I gave my informer the automatic. It was a useless weapon but was the one item he had inquired about, and I had an idea he had secretly admired it before. He was delighted and offered to watch our house carefully for us from then on. We had no further trouble, but the story leaked out around town and the two housebreakers were in disgrace.

On the way back to camp the next afternoon, I approached the remains of the dead deer I had seen on the lake coming down. A black fox vainly hunted for a missed fragment of food and trotted off about thirty yards and sat down as I passed. He must have sensed I was unarmed and sat on his haunches looking at me as saucy as could be. I stopped and walked toward him, and he trotted off another twenty yards and sat down again, wrinkling his jowls in much the same manner as a friendly dog. He looked for all the world as though he were laughing at me. I yelled and waved my arms, but he wouldn't move until I again came closer. Tiring of my experiment, I stepped back into the toboggan harness and continued on my way. The fox then returned to his futile searching.

Between the two shacks, I had out two hundred and seventy traps. To visit them all every two weeks meant thirty miles a day of hard travel. Beaver had to be thawed out over a campfire and skinned on the trail, as some of the carcasses weighed as much as eighty pounds. The smaller animals I always packed in for skinning in the more comfortable surroundings of a warm cabin. Night after night, darkness would catch me with three to five hundred pounds of beaver carcasses still unskinned and up to twenty miles to my nearest camp. All I could do was make the best of it and pitch camp on the spot to finish the skinning in the morning. It was not an ordeal to cringe from and many times turned into a pleasant experience. The Indians had taught me the simplest methods of self-preservation under these circumstances and it was easy to find a sheltered spot, shovel away the snow with a snowshoe, and erect a form-fitting pup tent of spruce and balsam boughs open at the end that faced my fire. I would shovel the snow back again over the shelter, producing an impromptu airtight igloo that protected me from the elements. A spring bed of boughs from the same trees, laid tip up against a head log on the ground inside, furnished solid comfort. The heat from my supper fire warmed the interior, and at bedtime I worked myself feetfirst into the structure, fully clothed, and closed the open end with my packsack by pulling it tightly into the aperture after me. I was then as snug as a moth in a blanket.

I reset traps, changed unprofitable locations, and watched for new signs of fur movement in the snow. It was deep enough now so that snowshoes were a necessity, and I broke new trails along the line of my traps and had regular stops like a city postman. There would be the mouth of a creek, and along its winding route a falls or a rapids where game would be apt to feed; a beaver colony on one of the lakes; a point of swamp which all of the high land animals skirted and where fisher stopped to chase an occasional snowshoe rabbit; and ridges and thickets where the larger animals hunted and bedded down for the night.

I had an overwhelming desire to catch a fisher, and I know now that I wasted many unnecessary traps and hours of work on the scarce and cunning animals. I built cubbies on every point of swamp in the territory, baited them carefully, and set my traps according to the best advice from both the town and the Indian village. All that fell into them were flying squirrels, one weasel, and an American jay.

One day, on a shortcut, I ran across a week-old fisher track. It was the only one I had ever observed in all my miles of travels in the snow. I was elated. The track was on high ground, and I immediately took up the trail, dropping everything but two traps, my ax, and some bait. The fisher disdainfully passed up two swamps where I had set so carefully for him. I felt that, had the wind been right, he could not possibly have missed the odor of the delectable meals prepared and left there for him, for he passed well within a hundred yards of both sets; but on he went, mile upon mile. I looked forward to another night out, and this time without food. I had carelessly left a big piece of cold meat and some well-buttered bannock in my packsack back on the trail. The only food I had was a large square of milk chocolate that I always kept buttoned in the pocket of my wool shirt for just such an emergency. Finally the trail bore more to the south and then circled west. I did not know where I was, but at least he was now heading back more in the direction of our territory. We climbed onto still higher land, where the timber thinned out considerably. There could be nothing in this rocky desolation to interest an animal that fed on fish, rabbits, and small birds. I could not understand it, but then, just over a hill, the countryside dropped at a forty-five-degree angle from all sides into a deep pothole not seventy-five yards in diameter. It was covered with a dense growth of spruce and cedar, surrounded by marshy grass-covered hummocks. Fresh, well-used rabbit trails ran in every direction among the hummocks, and I discovered other fisher tracks that circled the edges of the swale. They were all about as old as the one I followed, and I could not be sure that they were not all made by the same animal. At least I had discovered his hunting ground.

This was as good a spot to spend the night as any, and I had plenty of time to reconnoiter and set my two traps to best advantage. I built three cubbies, two on the east side of the pothole at the farther end, close to the hummocks, which I set and baited with the utmost care. The bait was anchored with pointed sticks well at the back of the cubby, so it could not possibly fall on and spring the trap, which was sunk even with the ground five inches in front of the bait, the springs off to each side, the jaws opening perpendicular to the back log of the cubby and the pan directly in the center of the space between the two side logs. The logs of the cubby were tightly fitted and chinked with stone, so that there could be no possible entry to the bait except from the front and across the trap. For inches in front of the pan, I crossed two three-fourths-inch dry pointed limbs that I drove into the ground so that they would easily bear the weight of the animal without giving. The trap chain I pressed down close to one of the side logs and firmly drove the staple of the ring at the end of the chain into a short drag of green wood. The end of the chain, the ring, and the drag lay about a foot away from the cubby. All of these preparations I covered carefully inside the cubby with crumbled leaves, and outside with green spruce boughs. I was even careful not to leave any fresh ax cuttings or white branch ends exposed, so that all would look as natural as possible. When the set itself looked like a leafy floor, I covered over the cubby with more spruce boughs and laid a length of well-rotted log on top to block access from above.

Should a fisher choose to pay the cubby a visit, he would have to enter from the front, step on the crossed limbs, and, to get at the bait, take one more full step onto the raised pan of the trap. When the trap sprung from the weight of his foot on the pan, his leg would be fully extended and the jaws of the trap would close well above the first joint and hold him securely. The drag was heavy enough so that he could not go far, but it would allow him movement and progress that would keep him from giving up and chewing off his leg, the very thing that would happen if the trap were held to a stationary post. At the second set, I repeated the procedure.

The third cubby I placed at the center of the west side of the pothole, well inside the thick growth of spruce. I made this one man-sized and covered it with snow; it was to be my own shelter for the night. When I had eaten half of my chocolate bar, I crawled in and went to bed. The rest of my chocolate disappeared in the morning, and I was so hungry I could have taken on a fair-sized slab of bacon in addition, just for a filler. After one more careful inspection of the fisher sets, I set off with the sun on my back in the direction of camp. In five minutes or less, I was back on my trapline. I marked the spot by breaking down some bushes across the trail. It took me better than half an hour to backtrack to my packsack, but right there and then, I built a fire, made tea, and finished my cold meat and bannock. For days I had passed within spitting distance of a fisher's paradise, ignorant of its presence.

These animals are very dependable. They travel a regular route, keeping constantly on the move, but, almost to the day, you can bank on their returning to the same spot at eighteen-day intervals. I figured I had about eleven days to wait. Several times I was tempted just to take a peek but held myself back for fear I might get there on the fatal day and throw everything out of kilter. On the twelfth day, I hustled along to the brink of the pothole and then approached cautiously. There had been a disturbance at the first set; the cubby was torn apart. Full of excitement, I ran up and knelt down. The trap was gone. We had had a light snow, and it was difficult to see any other disturbance. I started to make small concentric circles, inspecting particularly any sign of brush that might have entangled the trap or drag. There was my fisher, not twenty feet away, chain and drag wound up in some scraggly bush. He was a grizzly old fellow, gray about the head and shoulders and silvered down the back, not a good specimen at all, but he was my first fisher, and I was as proud as a new father. Animals trapped this way do not suffer long. Struggling for release, they become exhausted and overheated, and freeze to death very quickly. This pothole brought me four more of much better quality during the balance of the winter.

My lines were now worked out in a cloverleaf pattern that covered the strategic points and returned me at the end of each day to the vicinity of my cabin. On my regular route, before the snows came, I had noticed an uprooted tree that seemed to collect an unusual quantity of dry leaves in the hollow beneath it. Each trip the leaves piled higher, and I suspected they had not all blown in with the wind. The snows had come, and as I passed the symmetrical mound that blanketed my tree, I stopped to investigate. A faint wisp of steam curled from the small aperture at its apex, which partially confirmed my suspicions. My gun was at the cabin, but I found a long dry branch and poked it down through the snow to the center where I had last seen the pile of leaves. There was a low guttural growl and I hastily backed away down the trail. I tipped my hat in mock apology and said in a low whisper, "Beg your pardon, old-timer, beg your pardon all to hell. Sorry to have disturbed you," and kept on going. I promised myself a nice bear rug when conditions were more in my favor, and planned on carrying my rifle on the next trip around. The exigencies of the traplines kept me and my mind occupied, and I never did get around to carrying a rifle on that route. Bruin slept on through his hibernation to a happy awakening in the warm spring sunshine.

It was a joy to be out in the sunny, soot-free, snow-blanketed wonderland, to be greeted in the morning by a cheery "chick-a-dee-dee-dee" from these gray-feathered little creatures that hunt larvae in the cracks of the trees along the trail, or to be waylaid by an inquisitive bandit whiskey jack. These birds are also known as lumberjacks, moosebirds, or Canada jays, and seem to appear from nowhere. They are very tame and watch the trails for an occasional scrap or crust of bread purposely dropped by passersby.

From my observations, Bill had not done a great deal of trapping, and I surmised that a large share of his time had been spent at the Indian village. There were at the head-quarters shack, however, in the neighborhood of thirty pelts, all told, that belonged to him. He did have one large, beautiful black otter pelt which I envied him. Though I had found otter signs and set my traps carefully, I had not been fortunate enough to bring in a single pelt from these beautiful animals. This fortunate and thrilling experience was in reserve for me in my later travels through the snow country.

When I spread out my traplines, I had found a promising creek ten feet wide on which I had made some mink sets. On this particular sunny afternoon, I was ahead of schedule and broke new trail further along up the bank of the stream, where I discovered another beaver dam. The snow blanketed the entire face of the dam down to the bed of the creek below at a forty-five-degree angle, and as I approached, a coal-black animal slid swiftly down the incline, then another one. "Otter," I breathed. They rolled and played in the snow, disappeared into the face of the dam, popped out and reappeared on the crest, and came hurtling down their slide again. I counted four of them before I interrupted their fun. When they saw me, they pricked up their tiny ears for a moment, raised their heads inquisitively, and then whipped out of sight with amazing speed. The dam was literally riddled with holes, and there were two slick slides to the deep water above. It was an ideal set, and I plugged into the dam about four inches underwater some beaver cuttings on which to set my trap. There was no need for bait in this natural runway. I set two more below the dam and one a short way above, beneath an overhanging bank.

It was three days before I got back. At the hole into the pond, I had caught a big fellow, the daddy of them all. Below the dam a young one still struggled to free himself from the cruel jaws of my trap. I put him out of his misery and raised the two of them up in front of me to admire the coal-black sheen of their guard hair and the beautiful pearl gray of the underfur. I had finally caught my otter, and not one, but two. There did not seem to be any beaver left in the pond above the dam and I did not catch any more otter there either. It did, however, become a very good mink spot that brought in several fine hides on future visits.

Christmas is the trappers' day of days, and the beginning of two weeks of festivities in the village. Many spring their traps and cease operations through the bitter cold of the first two months of the year, when even the wildlife holes up for a short period of hibernation. Others leave their sets and visit them weekly, picking up the few stragglers that are brave enough to sally forth on the sunny days for a brief inspection, but from Christmas to New Year's the woods are practically deserted. It is a period of joyful reunions. The saloons and village stores are full of woodsmen, drinking, buying supplies, swapping yarns, trading experiences, proudly displaying choice pelts, and discussing the spring operations. Some blow their entire fall stake in riotous living and return to their labors with nothing to show for their days of grueling toil.

I left my traps set and planned to return after the holiday. There was more of interest to me in the woods than in town, and Bill and I had prepared well, early in the fall, for a winter of solid comfort and genteel living in our homely hideaways.

On my way in, I followed one of the traplines that led toward town and looked in on some wolf sets made before the snows, along a heavily timbered ridge. The first one was hopelessly buried. By a twist of ill luck, the winds had swirled down through a nearby opening in the foliage and deposited four feet of snow over the trap. However, the lungs of a deer which I had used for bait were gone. This was interesting if not profitable, and I proceeded down the ridge with more caution.

At the next set, there had recently been a considerable disturbance. The crusted snows were torn up into little blocks all over the area, and previously buried fronds of ground hemlock stuck their green foliage through the white covering. Slowly I circled the spot at a safe distance, watching for a dirty gray patch of fur or a sign on the snow that my heavy drag had been pulled down the embankment. I could see my bait still in the crotch of a tree where I had placed it. Crossing over the ridge on the far side, I started circling back again. There wasn't a sign. I cut up closer to the disturbed area to avoid a thicket of low-lying evergreens, carefully watching for any signs of broken crust that would indicate my quarry had taken refuge in this thick cover. There wasn't a scratch on the frozen surface. As I passed the nearest point of small bushes, my backbone did a quick freeze that started at my tailbone and ran up on into my neck and shoulders. There had been a vicious, deep-throated bass growl that sounded as though it originated in my hip pocket. I ran up the hill without even looking back, and I could feel the hot breath of my imagined pursuer on the seat of my pants as I scrambled for a foothold. My only means of protection was the small ax safely enclosed in its leather case and strapped to the back of my packsack, about as handy and useful as my gun back at the cabin.

As I reached the top, I looked over my shoulder. I was not being followed by any flame-breathing dragon, nor by anything else that I could discover. My pack came off in a hurry, and I took my ax out of its case and cut a short maple cudgel about three inches in diameter almost before I realized what I was doing. I didn't even know the nature of the danger that confronted me, and here I was preparing in the prescribed manner to kill a trapped timber wolf. I wasn't even sure that I cared to tackle one if that were the source of my ominous warning.

Finally my teeth stopped chattering and my hands trembled only slightly. I could now survey the situation with some degree of clarity. The evergreen growth was just below me, but I could see no sign of life. With my short club in my right hand for a quick blow and my double-bitted ax clutched to the blade in my left for action in case of closer quarters, I decided to reconnoiter. Walking down the ridge to where I had crossed below my trap, I dropped down even with the center of the cover I had so recently fled from. I approached with care, dropping on one knee every few feet to peer beneath the foliage. It was as dark as a cavern in there, and I was getting too close for comfort. Backing up a few feet, I tore some dead bark from a stub and threw the pieces into the likeliest-looking places for an animal to hide. At every throw, new chills chased each other over my nervous system, but there were no further warnings to be heard. It looked as though it would be necessary to again climb the ridge and have a try from the farther side, but as I started to turn, I caught the slight quiver of an evergreen out of the corner of my eye on the low side of the patch, some thirty feet below me. Ripping off an extra-large chunk of bark, I heaved it at the spot where the tree had been in motion. Immediately the little clump whipped and wavered as if in a gale of wind, and ugly snarls rolled up the hill to sound as if they came from right at my feet. When the commotion died down and my pulse returned to normal, I made my way to a spot a little above the level of the disturbance and once again closed in— peering intently beneath the boughs of spruce and cedar. It was no use. I could imagine the contour of a body lying in the thicket and could produce an ominous growl at every cast of bark or branch, but it was too dangerous to approach any closer to an unseen foe until I knew he was securely held by both the trap and the drag it was attached to.

Climbing the hill, I skirted the thicket again. Where the trees protected the snow from the wind, the crust was much firmer. I found scratches on the surface that I had missed before and could picture what had happened. At the snap of the trap's jaw, the animal bolted for cover, skidding the drag endwise down the sharp incline close at his heels. In this position, it had failed to catch in the small trees, and he had almost reached the farther side of the thicket. When I had moved on up the trail, I again descended the ridge and worked back from the opposite side of the small cluster of trees. At the edge of the last grouping, there he was, squatting on his belly, one forefoot extended out in front of him. He was an enormous fellow, his eyes glaring ferociously, his mouth hanging open, baring vicious-looking teeth and his tongue hanging out in a pink curl as he panted from his exertions, breathing little clouds of frosty vapor into the still air. He gave several cringing tugs and I could see the trap and follow the line of the chain to the bushes that had entangled the drag. At sight of me, he backed into the cover, low rumblings issuing from his throat. This was just what I wanted. The chain circled the edge of the trees and stopped his retreat. I could see the front of his head and the extended forepaw plainly now. The jaws had closed above the dewclaws and he was firmly held. Before proceeding further, it was necessary to determine that the drag was also secure, and I worked up and around him for that purpose. As I had surmised, the drag had catapulted down the hill and entered the last bunch of seedlings end first. The frightened wolf, for faster flight, had turned aside, avoiding the bushes, and when the chain brought him up with a jerk it twisted the drag sideways, and it was firmly lodged between the small trees.

Finding a small sapling about fifteen feet long, I cut and trimmed it and pointed the small end. My ax I abandoned but kept within easy reach in case of emergency. With my new weapon in my left hand and my cudgel raised over my head for action, I now approached cautiously. The wolf retreated as far as he could and lunged backwards frantically. I watched the trap and chain for any signs of give and extended my sapling toward him until I was within striking distance. He alternately watched me intently through the black shuttle-like slits in his cold, expressionless yellow eyes and plunged wildly backwards in a last desperate effort to free himself, snarling and growling and snapping at my extended lance repeatedly. I jabbed him with the point of the stick at every opportunity until his fear finally gave way to anger at this new tormentor. Finally he came out of the bushes in a wild lunge, but the trap brought him up short and tripped him. He was on his feet in an instant, growling and snarling his protest, the hair on the scruff of his neck bristling in a threatening manner, but I had now determined how far he could lunge toward me, and I narrowed the distance between us while he strained to reach me. He tore at my goad and cut a good six inches off the end with his sharp, powerful fangs. I was almost ready to strike. If anything went wrong now, I would have to act quicker than he did, as I was within four feet of his slathering, snapping pink jaws. I jabbed him again with my sapling; he strained at the chain. "Now!" I thought, and brought my club down swiftly on his skull with all my strength. There was a loud crack and he crumpled in the snow. I rushed in and struck two more well-placed blows to be sure he would not get up and come for me again. I had trapped my first timber wolf, and the hide would back the story of his size when I told it in the village.

It was the day before Christmas when I arrived in town. Bill was already at the town house. I took my fur directly to

Mr. [Chris. C.] Smith, the lumber company's caretaker who bought fur as a sideline in the winter, and came away with a check for twelve hundred dollars. He couldn't believe his eyes when he saw a greenhorn's catch that amounted to that kind of money, but I felt I had been treated fairly. Mrs. [Rose] Smith invited me to Christmas dinner in the bargain, and I accepted promptly, for I knew I would be a little homesick at not being with my parents on this holiday. There were several wrapped Christmas packages at the post office for me, and a stack of letters, mostly from my dear mother, who never failed to send her weekly note of guidance and cheer. Mr. Smith broadcast my success to the other trappers who brought their pelts to him, and they all dropped in to congratulate me on my prowess as a sourdough.

The Johnson boys,* who ran a canoe livery and a tourists' launch on the first lake, arrived at the house soon after I got back. They had heard of my catch and also of the trouble with Bill. I knew that, in the spring, I would not be able to keep up the pace single-handed, when beaver trapping started in earnest, and I invited the older Johnson boy, Oscar, to join me on a fifty-fifty basis. He was delighted with the chance, as he had been planning to trap someplace, and this was a ready-made opportunity.

Bill was quite congenial, and we had many of our mutual friends in for a meal or a spot of Christmas cheer during our stay. For a Christmas Eve supper, we had thick, juicy moose steaks brought down from headquarters. As we were about

* Oscar and William Johnson, ages twenty-eight and thirty, are listed in the 1920 census, along with three other sons, in Charles A. Johnson's Winton household.

to sit down, there was a knock on the door. The game warden, Jim O'Connell, had beaten his way up the street through too many swinging doors and now, weaving uncertainly, stood on our threshold. He was a good friend of Bill's, but we didn't know what to do, nor what direction his inebriation might take. If he remained pleasant, we were sure he would ignore the moose steaks, but if it turned ugly, no telling what might happen. Bill offered him a drink, which he refused. He did not want to go home on Christmas Eve in his condition and had taken refuge at our house for a chance to sober up, so we decided to invite him in for supper. The first thing he did was to pour himself a coffee cup full of cider vinegar, straight, which he downed without a whimper. He said it was wonderful to sober up on, but I choked for him as I watched it disappear. He chewed away on a great slab of steak without registering what he was eating, and our fears subsided. In the course of our conversation, he promised to visit headquarters camp after the holidays. The meal or the vinegar did a good job, and shortly after dinner he stumbled from our steps for home.

Early Christmas morning, we had another visitor. Leo Chosa dropped in and outlined a fur-buying trip he planned for after the first of the year, asking permission to make our headquarters camp his first overnight stop. We were glad to extend him an invitation. He was making a big circle of the lakes to the north, replenishing his supplies at Cowin,* a small town on the Canadian Northern Railway, some three hundred and fifty miles distant. He had a good team of

* Cook probably meant Cowan, a village some two hundred miles northwest of Winnipeg, Manitoba.

twelve dogs, and I sprouted the idea of making the trip with him just to see the country. The suggestion that he ought to have me along for company was well received, but he explained that the trip was a tough one and insisted I would not be able to stand it. I told him I could take anything he could, and was so eager that he finally consented. He warned me that the trip was his bread and butter, and, should I play out, he would have to leave me to make my own way back to civilization as best I could. It was a fifty-fifty deal on food. Leo was a little short of money, but he wanted to buy all the fur he could first; after that I was to buy if the dogsled would hold any more.

We made out a list of groceries and, as far as I could see, we were going to exist on salt pork and bannock the entire trip. He turned down my suggestion of a few prunes, some sugar, and a little butter. "Too heavy," he explained. If he could take it, I could too, and I gave him no argument. It was agreed that I would meet him at headquarters on January 3. He would get the supplies before he left, and I would pay for half of our food when he arrived. In the meantime, I planned to return to my trapline and prepare for a two-month holiday. I was so excited I could hardly contain myself. Two months in the interior by dog team with a mixed-blood, a trapper and woodsman par excellence, were beyond my wildest dreams of good fortune.

I left for camp on December 27 and raced around my traplines. I stored away everything, and swung bedding and clothing from the rafters by haywire, away from the mice. I packed my pelts to leave at headquarters and carefully went over the small items I wished to take with me.

On December 31 I sprung my traps, picked up my fur, and pulled into headquarters. Bill had come up the day after I left town, but Leo did not arrive until about nine o'clock that night. Far down the trail, I heard the tinkle of the little bells that each dog wore on his collar.

I have seen it with my own eyes a dozen times, and I still can't believe that twelve dogs averaging around seventy pounds apiece can pull a dogsled loaded with twelve hundred pounds of provisions. Leo's load was mostly salt pork, flour, and calico. There were a few dozen heavy wool socks, a sack of rice, some beans, and a little box of bright-colored trinkets. Leo unhooked the dogs and tied them separately to any object he could find that would not allow them to get together in the night and start a fight, and came in for supper.

After the meal, we fed the dogs a good ration from our supply of frozen trap bait, and I threw in for good measure all of the table scraps and the remains of our venison roast. Leo went over the list of what I planned to take along, culled out here, and added a necessity there. We were to travel with only one blanket apiece in weather that might any minute drop beyond fifty degrees below zero. I pictured myself unrolling bolts of calico and wrapping myself in swaths of the material to keep warm. At the last minute, I could not bring myself to leave without smuggling into my packsack a few pounds of prunes in the event I needed a laxative, and a small sack of sugar for my tea. Later on, Leo acknowledged the pleasure and change these two luxuries afforded us. I concluded that leaving them out in the first place had been an act to show me how tough and hard-boiled a real sourdough really was. We did take some starter from our sourdough pail also, and I packed the ball of dough next to my back for warmth while we were on the trail, sleeping with it at night rolled up with me in my blanket to keep the bacteria alive and working in the freezing cold weather.

We planned to be on our way at four-thirty the next morning. When I went down to the lake for a pail of water, the air was much colder, and the dogs were all rolled into tight little balls, their feet and noses buried in their soft bellies, their tails drawn in snugly around them for a covering. One bright eye peeked out inquiringly from each motionless mound, but they did not rouse until I brought out the breakfast scraps. Leo fed them their three-and-one-half pound daily ration of frozen fish, then checked the load and inspected the harness while the dogs ate and growled their warnings as the faster eaters strained covetously in the direction of those who had not yet finished their meal. We hooked up the team and at a "mush" from Leo, they started on the long trail.

He used a stout single lead line, connected to the drawbar of the sled, to which the dogs were alternately attached by a single tug snapped onto their sheepskin-lined collars from between their forelegs. There was only one thoroughbred husky in the team, and with due respect for the breed, I must say that she was the poorest dog of the lot. The rest of them were an untraceable mixture, Newfoundland, Airedale, and husky strains predominating. Nero, the lead dog, was a character and an invaluable asset and example for the rest of the team. He never faltered and burned up the miles tirelessly while on the trail. An aloof individual, he held himself above the rest of the team like an army major, keeping order among his charges by diving into any fight and throwing the aggressors twenty feet in opposite directions in his powerful jaws. He was a willing worker and pulled more than his share in the harness, besides knowing the routes as well as Leo did himself, and it was astounding to watch his intelligent actions as he met the problems of the day. If it was to be a long, grueling day, he would start slowly and settle down into a dogged, mile-consuming pace that would conserve his and the team's strength to the end. On a short trip, he would snap into the harness and literally jerk the team off their feet, carrying both them and the sled with him in his eagerness. He knew it meant a longer rest at the other end. On return trips, Nero was even more ambitious, and the last day into town was always an ordeal for Leo, who had to dogtrot himself to keep up with his excited wards.

As if to assist Leo in my initiation, the temperature dropped steadily all day. It was bitter cold, and I looked forward to the night and my one little wool blanket with many misgivings. Around four o'clock, Nero slackened his pace, and at a big swamp that came down to the lake on which we were traveling, he edged in close to the timber, stopped, and looked back inquiringly. Leo went up ahead and turned in among the spruce. He was back in a few minutes and with the command "haw," we followed his snowshoe trail and disappeared in to the heavy growth of evergreens.

Forty yards in from the lake, we stopped at a spot some twenty feet in diameter, completely free of trees and brush, the ground covered with a lush growth of marsh grass under the snow. We were completely closed in on all sides by thick spruce and balsam. The dogs lay down in their harness, biting the balled-up ice from between their toes while they waited for Leo to unharness them. I shoveled out the area with my snowshoes, throwing snow into the surrounding trees, banking and closing the space beneath the evergreens where there were no branches. We built a fire at the edge of the clearing where we had clipped off the branches on the side of the trees nearest us, so that they would not catch, and stomped out the burning marsh grass for a safe distance around it. I had not realized it until we were done with these labors, but I was actually perspiring, and our little green-walled room with the blue-sky ceiling was as warm and comfortable as a steam-heated apartment. It seemed cruel to tether the dogs to the bushes, but we were still close enough to town so that we knew, with the exception of Nero, they would all head for home if we allowed them to roam at will. While I cooked our supper, Leo cut a pile of green wood with which to bank our fire for the night, lopping off the spruce boughs for our bed. At the last moment the green wood was piled tightly over the coals of our fire and, rolled up in our blankets, feet toward the heat, our mackinaws for pillows, we went to sleep. Dogs and men were comfortably disposed about the clearing. Toward morning, I awoke and found that, as the fire died down, the dogs had crept in closer for more warmth, and we were all in one little huddle. It was my first experience sleeping with the dogs, but I found that it added to our comfort as well as theirs. I got up and threw more wood on the fire and did not awaken again until I could smell the frying salt pork. I missed my morning coffee for the first few days, but eventually looked forward to a cup of hot tea with fully as much relish.

The night before, I had tied a small thermometer to a spruce at the edge of the lake. It stood at fifty-three below zero as we left, and it remained there for three full days. It did not seem possible that we were sleeping out in such weather with only one blanket apiece without freezing to death, but we were never the least bit uncomfortable. To be sure, I was chilly when I awakened in the early mornings, but no more so than I had been many times in my own room at home. The depth of the swamp, the snow-banked opening in the trees, and the fact that the wind could not penetrate the thick foliage around us was the secret of our warmth, the glowing embers of our all-night fire adding their cheery heat to our cozy retreat.

The first commercial stop was made the next night at the birch-bark-covered teepee of Joe Blackbird and his wife. Leo told me it would not be successful, but he did sell Mrs. Blackbird, for cash, a few yards of bright red calico that she could not resist. Among Joe's pelts were two top-quality fisher, beautifully furred out with long, silky coal-black guard hair covering an exceptionally heavy nap of rich, fluffy underfur. They were not for sale, but with Leo's permission and advice as to their worth, I offered Joe two hundred and fifty dollars for them. He was not even tempted. I learned that later, Frank Chosa had traded a gallon jug of moon, worth about a dollar, for both of them at the portage. When Joe sobered up, he made quite a fuss about the deal, but that was as far as it went, and Frank pocketed a handsome profit.

We were covering an average of forty miles per day, picking up a little fur here and unloading some of our provisions there to other Joes along our zigzag route. Periodically, we were forced to stop and fish for the dogs. It took fifty pounds per day to feed them, and it was quite a job to cut through four feet of ice and make a hole large enough for fishing, so at each stop, we loaded the sled as heavily as we dared and cut down these delaying labors to about every fifth day.

The weather turned warmer, and big thunderheads appeared along the horizon. Leo predicted snow. When we dug in for the night, the sky was completely overcast with a smoky indigo pall. The dogs were nervous and whined continuously. We prepared for trouble by building a lean-to of boughs over the spot where we would bed down, and we cut three times as much firewood as we expected to need, in addition to skidding in several good dry stubs handy to our camp. When we awoke in the morning, nothing much had happened except that a few lone snowflakes were beginning to fall. Leo decided to push on to a more acceptable campsite, just in case we were in for a blizzard. By midmorning it was snowing heavily, but the traveling was good, and we were nearing the camping spot Leo had in mind. At the north end of a huge lake, a grove of thickly growing white pine acted as a natural windbreaker for a dense swamp of cedar and spruce. On previous trips, Leo had fashioned and improved from time to time a semi-permanent wigwam-type shelter at this spot. There would be no snow in the wigwam, and an inside fire would keep us warm and dry.

The going got heavier, but two o'clock brought us to the last portage. We only had nine miles left to go. The moment we were well out on the ice, as if by a signal, and with the noise of a switch engine blowing off steam, the blast hit us from the northeast. It was necessary to turn our backs to it to get a deep breath. The dogs were bewildered and turned first one way and then the other to escape the stinging sleet which formed from the broken snowflakes. Leo gave the dogs their heads. Nero knew where he was going and pushed along bravely, head held close to the ground to avoid the icy blast. Time and again the team nearly threw him off his feet as they staggered along behind him. We kept a hand on the sled or bent closely over the dogs as we made frequent trips forward to inspect them, to be sure that we did not become separated from our little group. Our clothing and sled were a mass of ice, and the fine snow had matted in the fur of our team, so that even the heat of their exertions could not penetrate the icy mass. They were like white ghosts of the wilderness storm.

The sleet froze on our eyebrows and eyelashes and required constant attention to keep it from closing our eyes and blinding us. Leo and I both went forward and found every last one of the dogs completely blind. Thick coatings of ice had anchored to the fur around the eye sockets, completely bridging their eyeballs. We tried to break it loose, and the dogs whimpered pitifully as we pulled the frozen crystals from their hair. Our hands were nearly frozen. Leo made a quick decision and unhooked the lead line from the sled, holding onto Nero's collar. He called to me to get our packsacks of food and blankets, and as I did so, I threw in as much frozen fish as I dared to carry, and joined him. He had melted the ice from Nero's eyes and we headed for shore, dragging our blinded team behind the leader. We plodded along a short distance in wishful thinking that we might still be able to reach the camp. It was hopeless. Nero's eyes and our own were quickly frozen shut again.

We stumbled along to some low land and were fortunate
to find a small clump of scraggly cedars that at least afforded
us some shelter. Leo quickly built a low windbreaker of short
boughs for our fire while I scouted for wood. The only thing
I could find was a dead cedar spike, but this would do for a
start. I couldn't see how, even with a windbreaker, Leo could
manage a fire in that gale of ice-filled air, but he shoveled
away the snow behind the bough barrier, laid the fire carefully with some dry curled shavings from one of the larger
sticks, covered himself completely with his blanket, and from
someplace produced a coach candle, which he lit with a
match. He now had a permanent flame he could hold under
the wood until it caught, at the same time conserving
matches for possible future emergencies. The wood sputtered
and burst into flame. We threw on everything I had gathered, which gave us enough light to get set, after a fashion,
for the night. Leo tied a stripped spruce to the branches of
the tree upwind from the fire and laid a heavy covering of
boughs, stems stuck in the snow, against it while I towed in
more wood exposed by the firelight. It was out of the question to dry out green wood as the embers of the fire blew
away almost before they became coals.

The sleet curled over our lean-to like the crest of a wave,
and before long had us sealed in from the front as well as the
back. It was just as well, for there was no heat from the fire
anyway. It burned more like a blowtorch, the flame standing
out straight to one side, noisily protesting the draft that all
but blew it out. We did get some snow tea, made and fried
some salt pork, but any kind of breadstuff was out of the
question in that wind. We closed in both ends of our crystal

palace, squared off a space for bough beds, and brought in a frying pan full of coals from our outside fire with which to start a new one. The blustering storm sealed up our burrow in no time, and we were at least resting in endurable discomfort, glad to be out of the stinging sleet. Leo would have allowed the dogs to wait out the storm without food, but I doubled their rations in acknowledgment of their brave efforts of the afternoon, hoping to furnish them with a little extra fuel with which to face the ordeal of another night in the snow, this time without shelter or the comforting warmth of a fire.

There was less snow in the air in the morning, but the wind continued to howl down from the north, crashing to earth huge trees that had stood for a hundred years and making a shambles of unprotected younger growths. We could not see our sled from the shore, but knew it could be nothing more than a white mound of drifted snow and ice. We decided to leave it where it stood and try to make Leo's old camp on the upper end of the lake where we would have room to turn around. It was a nasty trip, and even without a load to hamper their progress, the dogs shrunk from facing the blast. The wigwam was still standing and there was less than a foot of new snow in the lee of the tall pines.

Comparatively, this was solid comfort, except for the fact that we were running low on food. I had my ball of sourdough in a sack beneath my jumper, and there was sufficient flour for several days, but our meat and main supplies were buried six miles back under a mountain of drifting snow. There was no place to go, and nothing to do even if you could get there. We cut another hole in the ice and fished for dog food behind several Christmas trees which we set up for protection from the wind. All that day and the next, the storm protested our presence. We fed on dough gods, chunks of biscuit dough the size of a man's fist, pressed around green twigs and baked by rotating them in the heat of our fire. We ate dog food too—fresh-caught northerns, grilled to a tempting brown, were not to be cast aside as food unfit for human consumption, at least not by hungry travelers in our predicament. We did not fare badly, however, and with flapjacks, fried pork, and hot tea for breakfasts, we could have stayed a week. The dogs had done nothing but eat and sleep for two days, and like ourselves were restless and ready to push on.

The fourth day of our imprisonment came off crisp and sunny. Returning to the sled, we saw nothing but an elongated mound of glazed-over snow and ice. Even our tracks were entirely obliterated. We had nothing for shovels but our snowshoes, and the sharp, frozen crystals bit into the frames, ruining a pair for both of us. Finally we got down to where we could rock the load, and we broke all the runners loose. The dogs jumped into the harness with a will, and together we pulled the sled free. Our case knives carved off the sharp protruding ice that clung to the runners, and scratching and clawing for a foothold on the slipping surface of the snow, the dogs took up the trail again, as happy as we were in getting back to work again.

Night found us camped twenty miles beyond the scene of our incarceration, where we broke out our supplies and dined on a haunch of well-seasoned venison, our first good meal in a week. In a complete reversal, the air was now as clear as crystal, the horizon alight with shafts of shifting fire—reds, greens, blues, yellows, and incandescent whites, the beams roaming the heavens like giant searchlights on a battlefield. The trees of the forest snapped and groaned, shifting their positions with loud reports as they unloaded the snow from their heavily weighted boughs. I could imagine the sharp crack of rifle fire close by and the dull thud of exploding bombs in the distance as suddenly released flares of unusual intensity illuminated the universe. The northern lights were outdoing themselves in a dance of the rainbows, a sight beyond comprehension that eclipsed the most stupendous Fourth of July celebration that I had ever witnessed. We stood there in awed silence watching their gyrations. It was truly a winter wonderland.

At the end of three weeks, a dirty, bewhiskered pair mushed in to Cowin. It was only a whistle-stop, but there was a hotel where we engaged a room for the night. I took my first Finnish bath that afternoon at a community bathhouse, and how good it felt. We stepped into a warm shower, soaped and scrubbed until our bodies were pink, and then sat on long benches in the steam room, slapping ourselves all over with prepared bunches of sweet-scented cedar fronds that left us feeling immaculately clean and delicately scented. The Finns end their ablutions with a quick plunge into an ice-cold shower, or a naked roll in a snowbank, but that sounded rather rugged to me, and I had had enough of cold and snow already to last me for some time to come. We were content to cool down to normal in the waiting room before going back to the hotel.

We replenished our supplies, sorted our pelts by species and packed them into gunnysacks, tying our load securely to the sled. There was nothing to do here, and the half-buried shanties, put to bed for the winter under their blanket of snow, smoke curling from their stovepipe chimneys, was about all there was to see. The longest leg of our journey still lay ahead, and early in the morning we headed west to meet another string of lakes that we would follow on the return trip.

I don't know why I was so intrigued by this trip. There was nothing but hard work, rations limited to the utter necessities, cold, snow, and blizzards to keep us company, and an unlimited ghostlike wilderness, stark and still in its majesty, to travel through, but I loved every moment of it. The tinkling bells on the dogs, the hissing of the sled runners, the "slough, slough, slough" of Leo's snowshoes breaking trail up ahead were all accompaniment to our progress. The only life we saw was an occasional croaking raven, chickadees, whisky jacks, downy woodpeckers, and two great American woodpeckers—a bird that is now almost extinct.* We did see deer that crossed the narrows between lakes on two different occasions, but that was all. Even the game preferred their shelters to the biting cold, whistling winds, and drifting snow of the open lakes. It was a world of emptiness, of broad expanse, unfathomable depths, and silence, silence that you stopped and listened for but did not hear, yet it bore in on you from all sides and engulfed you with its enormity, leaving you breathless and awed by its crushing weight.

Each day we were getting closer to home. The sled bulged with pelts. Leo had run out of money, and he had almost

---

* Cook probably saw two pileated woodpeckers.

exhausted his supply of trade goods. I was buying most of the fur now, judging its quality under Leo's practiced eye. We were nearing a full load and would soon have to stop trading. The dogs took on new life as the landmarks became more familiar. They pricked up their ears and lengthened their stride, their bright eyes shining in anticipation of a long rest as they sensed the end of the journey.

On the last night out, during supper, Leo told me we were sixty-five miles from town and asked, "Do you think you can make it?" I nearly choked on a fish bone. Covering forty miles a day, I had been asleep each night almost before I could drape my tired form around the obstructions that stuck through my hastily prepared bough mattresses. My reply, "I can make it if you can," sounded hollow and boastful, but I was willing to try.

We got off at four in the morning. I had stoked away all the salt pork and flapjacks I could hold against the endurance test ahead of us. The dogs tested our mettle, pushing on faster, ever faster, without any urging from the driver. I was dead tired at noon and reclining during our lunch to gain back all of the reserve energy possible before pushing on. We had run into minor difficulties all day. The portage crossings were four and five feet deep in snow. The dogs sunk in and floundered around in their effort to obtain a pulling foothold. We put our shoulders to the load and helped them through time after time. Intervals between spurts were more frequent now, and each time we rested, I wondered how I could possibly get to my feet again. Leo was visibly tired too. The dogs' tails drooped and their heads hung low, but they would not give in; by this time, they could scent familiar surroundings and anticipate a good meal and a long, uninterrupted sleep.

We reached portage at the last lake just at dark. To our consternation, the lake level had fallen recently, and just that day the ice had broken from the shore and dropped down several inches into the water. For thirty feet out along the entire perimeter, there were four or five inches of wet, unfrozen slush. We looked in vain for a dry runway onto the lake. This meant ice balling up between the dogs' toes and cutting them cruelly, and endless stops to remove these hindrances. It meant crusted sled runners and wet moccasins. There was nothing to do but wade into it; no one gave a thought to spending the night just eighteen miles from town. I judged the temperature at eighteen below. It was twenty-two below by the thermometer on the sled when I checked it after supper. Two quarts of hot tea had revived me, though good, solid food would have been much wiser. We pushed onto the ice and, after wading through the slush, dried fifty-two soaked feet with all the spare bandannas, used and otherwise, that we could muster, before going on. Water had gone over the tops of my tightly laced moccasins, and five pair of heavy woolen socks were cold and clammy. I hoped they would dry as we moved along.

The dogs were flying and Leo took off his snowshoes, hung onto the sled handles, and fudged a little bit now and then by riding the runners when the pace became too fast for him. I wanted to tell Leo that I could go no further, for I was completely done in and had used up the last ounce of my vitality. I began to lag behind, but Leo was the first to ask for quarter. He yelled back from the load that he was all in and was going to ride the sled the balance of the way into town. Before I could muster the strength to call and tell him that I too had reached the end of my endurance, the dogs had surged ahead and he was beyond recall.

I could see the lights of the village ahead of me now, I judged about eight miles away. I just couldn't make it. With that thought, I became panicky and lunged forward on the run for a few yards until I stumbled and fell, completely exhausted. I lay there for a moment and felt my taut raw muscles slowly relax. A warm, comfortable feeling slowly stole over my body and enveloped me. My brain ceased to function properly and my one desire seemed to be to let go of myself and drift off into peaceful slumber. I was slowly freezing to death. My body was wet with nervous perspiration, but I shook violently with the cold. I could hear my teeth chattering as they came together with the force of hammer blows, but the sound was far away. I felt I must get up, and yet the desire for sleep was almost overwhelming. Had I yielded, it would have been the end.

Just ahead of me, on a point, there was a summer cottage. I could see the outline against the star-lit sky through my semi-consciousness. If I could only make it, I could build a fire and rest for a moment. There might even be coffee in the cupboard. It was the thought of the coffee that did it, and I struggled to my feet again. At least I could heat some water and start my blood to circulating. I could hardly keep my eyes open, but knew I was facing death if I gave in. Somehow, I aroused sufficiently to make the shelter. It was open and I kicked off my snowshoes and walked in. The blood was oozing through my moose-hide moccasins where the frozen mule-hide snowshoe lacings had cut through my five pair of sodden wool socks. There was no wood, and not even a scrap of paper in the shack. I managed to stumble out again and collected a pitiful handful of dry twigs from around the building. I knocked a leg off the table with a chair, broke it into stove lengths, and tried to start a fire. I couldn't even feel the match flame held against my fingers. I cupped the next one in my hands and let it burn out, absorbing what little heat I could from the weak flame. I then placed my twigs in the stove and held a lighted match underneath them. They caught for a moment and then sputtered out. I lit another match and laid it on the twigs and threw in all the matches I had. They flared up one at a time, as the sulfur caught, and I held the chair leg and both hands in the flames at the same time in hopes that the heavier table leg would catch and give me more warmth, but the twigs and matches burned down and went out.

I remember leaving the shack a little warmer for having been out of the wind and from the heat of the matches I had burned. The feeling was back in my hands, they were warm again, and for the moment my senses had returned. The last six miles to town are a complete blank to this day. How I ever got there is a miracle. Luckily Bill was at the town house when I stumbled in about ten o'clock. He could see I was more dead than alive and poured two cups of black coffee into me immediately, undressed me, and put me to bed. When I woke up, at two the next afternoon, I couldn't even remember how I got there.

Bill had gone over to Leo's in the morning while I still slept and found Leo in bed with a high fever. He remained there for four days, hovering on the verge of pneumonia, but heat and food brought him around, also. He got a lot of fun afterwards out of telling how a tenderfoot had beaten him at his own game, but I never quite forgave him for leaving me out there on the lake to freeze to death.

THE REAL COLD WEATHER WAS OVER. I had been gone just two months, and after two days' recuperation prepared to leave for camp. Bill decided to go along, and we spent the night at headquarters. He was unusually amiable, and I planned on visiting him often from then on; I felt sorry for this good-hearted, lonesome soul and hoped to renew the old friendly relations.

Urgent business awaited me at my camps. My traps had remained unset too long and I set out the next morning, my first stop O'Niel's cabin. There was now around five feet of snow on the level in the woods and it was tough going, even on snowshoes, where no trail had been broken. I was fresh, however, and took a beeline shortcut through the heavy timber to save myself a few miles and get a change of scenery. The sun had not penetrated the heavy hemlock foliage, and I came up with a shovelful of snow on the front of my snowshoes at every step. I began to regret my laziness and was puffing heavily in the first ten miles. One of our trails skirted the timber on the farther side and I thought I could save time and effort by cutting over to it.

Around Christmastime, a dozen or more deer had yarded up near the trail just inside the tall timber, in anticipation of the heavy snows. I had seen them once from a distance on my way down. Here they could stamp down the snow over a large area by milling about and keep available the low bushes and ground hemlock that would pull them through while the snow was too deep and soft for them to travel. I thought I could hit the trail just above it, but I missed by about a mile and landed right at the yard. It was a bloody sight. Fur and lower front legs were strewn everywhere. You could see where the animals had lunged at the walls of their prison, only to bury themselves in the snow, where they had struggled and fallen back again. There were faint trails of pink in all directions where the wolves had dragged small portions of meat over the snow. It must have been a large pack to raise such havoc and carry off at least a ton of meat without leaving so much as a vestige of a carcass behind. No wonder the deer population had failed to gain and overrun the country. I thought, "The survival of the fittest. Nature's way of maintaining a balance among her wild creatures."

Everything was just as I had left it, and I rebaited and reset along the entire route coming into camp. The bait left there when I had pulled my sets was all gone, and there were lots of signs of visitors as I made my rounds. The next two weeks were a harvest, mostly mink, and over the weekend I ran a load of fur down to headquarters. Bill was there, feet up on the grindstone, smoking his old corncob and slowly rocking back and forth on the back legs of the cane and willow chair.

During the day, the weather had turned warm, and that night, over our pipes, we discussed the possibilities of an early spring thaw. Suddenly I could hear sleigh bells out of the past, dog bells from Leo's team. "I must be dreaming," I thought, but Bill had heard them too and told me Leo had passed through going east the morning before. We could not understand what had brought him back. I opened the door and looked. Enormous flakes of wet snow were falling gently, and there stood Leo and his team, heading down the trail toward town.

"Hi, there, old-timer," he called in friendly greeting. "Got a bed for an old buddy?"

"No, damn you, stay out there and freeze to death, like you nearly did me," I answered.

Leo laughed heartily. Life or death, what difference did it make to one who lived so dangerously? Daily, hand in hand, these two specters stalked his trail, the one giving joy and contentment, the nearness of the other furnishing the thrill and excitement that made living worthwhile.

"Bill tole me you nearly didn't make it," he went on, more soberly. "Jeez! I wouldn't a left ya if I'd known you were beat, too. I was done in when I went on ahead."

I could feel Leo's admiration of the stamina I had displayed on our trip, and his frank apology dissipated any resentment I may have felt over his desertion.

"Come on in, you bum. There's always room for one more," I called to him as I went for my jacket. I had to go out and shake hands with old Nero and take him a token of my esteem, a leftover meatball from our supper. Leo shouldered a large canvas-wrapped package from the sled and while I held the door open for him, he walked in, standing his load in the corner of our shack. "Whatcha got there?" I inquired.

"Take a look," he replied, jerking his head toward the

bundle as he went over to shake hands with Bill. I threw back the canvas and took a startled step backwards. I was looking straight into the sightless, staring eyes of a stiffly frozen corpse. The shock that this disclosure gave me afforded Leo another good laugh. He had started on his eastern route and stopped in at a cabin thirty miles above us to pass the time of day with a professor from an eastern college who had come up there two years before for his health. He was a tubercular who seemed to be doing nicely, getting out in the sun daily on snowshoes for long hikes and sleeping in the crisp, cold, northern woods air. The combination of these health-giving factors had brought him back a long way, and he had hoped to be able to leave in another year. There was plenty of wood and water in the shack, and no signs of injury on the corpse, so Leo had concluded that some form of sickness had caused his death. Possibly a relapse, during the cold snap that Leo and I had experienced, was his undoing. At any rate, he had died in his bed, where Leo had found him, the remnants of a meal still in the frying pan on the stove. I had met the man once but did not recognize his swollen, frost-covered face when I looked under the canvas. We took the body outside and hoisted it on the roof, where it would stay frozen and be safe from mice, and went to bed.

In the morning, Leo continued his gruesome trip to town and I returned to my traps. As I passed the narrows, I saw a lone female mallard winging up the lake. A hawk dove at her from an old dead pine stub, and by repeated dives forced her lower and lower until she floundered in the fresh snow on the lake, almost in front of me. The hawk closed in closer now, attacking in quick, short spurts. The mallard protected herself, flirting a wing at him at every dive, striking with her bony shoulder, but it was apparent he would soon have her exhausted and could then come in for the kill. I decided at this point to play good Samaritan, save a life, and deprive the hawk of his meal. He was plainly angry at my interference and made a few halfhearted dives at me before perching on a nearby tree. I only went close enough to scare the hawk off so the mallard would have time to recuperate. She did not rise while the hawk was present and seemed to recognize that I was her protector. Finally her attacker gave up in disgust and flew off. I waited a few moments and then approached closer to see if there had been any damage. When I was fifteen feet away, she got into the air and continued on up the lake. I recalled the flock of mallards I had reduced by seventy-five in the fall. The last time I had seen them, there were only about forty of the original three hundred left. Could it be that this lone hen was now the only survivor? This was another example of the law that I was fast being convinced ruled the wilderness: the survival of the fittest.

On the main route between the stopover and the headquarters shack there was a little creek, a mere trickle of water, that I had passed up many times as too small to bring results. This time I crossed the track of an exceptionally large mink and decided to investigate. Two hundred yards back in the brush, the mink track ended at a small opening in a beautifully constructed fourteen-foot-high beaver den, with a large pond behind it. This was the reason for the creek showing only a trickle of water. I set six traps on the way home and in the course of a week took out twelve beautiful coal-black beaver. Underneath their guard hair, the pelts showed an inch of beautiful, silver-sheened, powder-puff fur, as soft as a cotton boll. These were the most sought after type of beaver hide and would bring me premium prices from the buyers.

I also made a set for my mink below the dam and on my next visit found him in my trap, frozen under eight inches of ice. I chopped out a large section of the ice and carried his entombed carcass, trap and all, home in my packsack. When he had thawed out, he measured thirty-four inches of glistening black fur from tip to tip.

Jim O'Connell leaned back in my best chair, feet cocked up on the table, smoking, when I got back to the cabin, and there was a good fire in the cookstove.

"Isn't supper ready yet?" I greeted him.

"Hello, hello," he said, and then added, "I couldn't find where you hide your moose steaks."

We had told him about eating steaks with us at Christmastime, and he had taken it as a good joke on himself. "Guess you didn't look very hard," I told him. "Do you think you could stand another one?"

"I could eat a young bull all alone," he replied. There was a nice loin in my snowdrift refrigerator just outside the door. "Cut one to your size, and make mine about an inch thick," I told him.

While I got things ready, Jim cut the meat, and we sat down to a banquet. As we ate, he explained his mission and I agreed to go along with him for two days on one of his periodic inspection tours. Jim felt that as game warden, he had to at least make a gesture toward earning the money the state paid him. We sat and talked for a while and finally he said, "Someone's trappin' beaver on Prairie Lake. There ain't no timber floodin' there and that's agin the law." I could hardly hold my face straight; I had set traps at the beaver dam two days before, and I knew that a seasoned woodsman like Jim had undoubtedly followed my snowshoe trail from there right to my cabin. Then he said, "I hid a trap and a nice beaver in a fir on the east end of the dam. So whoever he is, he won't find it," and then looked at me with a knowing twinkle in his eye. All I said was, "Hmmm!"

We cut north and east toward Finn Charley's territory in the morning, loafing along and enjoying the sunshine. Charley Lokennen lived in town but maintained a camp on the border where he did a little sporadic trapping at the height of the seasons. His love for the bottle precluded any possibility of his ever becoming a threat to the fur-bearing population and I had paid him no attention. As Jim and I crossed on a high ridge between two lakes, we saw a figure on skis, crouched on the ice next to a beaver house. We approached noiselessly and stood directly above him, while Charley prepared to remove a beaver from one of his sets. When he stood up, beaver in hand, Jim cleared his throat. Charley dropped the beaver like a hot brick and attempted to kick it inconspicuously out of sight, but he had no cover in which to hide it. He was caught cold. "What you got there?" Jim asked.

Excitedly, Charley tried to talk himself out of his dilemma. "Hello, Yim," he called. "Some son of a gun rap beaver on my territory."

"Yeah? Bring it here," Jim called back. In dejected misery,

Charley labored up the steep bank. When he caught his breath, he said, "I no ketch him, Yim, I no rap beaver."

"No?" Jim said, and just stood there. Desperately, Charley tried to find a way out. The faster he talked, the more mixed up he became, and he jumbled his native Finnish and his English words so badly you couldn't understand a word he said. Finally, his face lit up. He couldn't pronounce any word that began with a *t* or a *d*, followed by an *r*, but he began hopefully, "You like good rink, Yim? I got good rink, you betcha." With that he fished around to his hip pocket and brought out a sixteen-ounce druggist's bottle three-quarters full of a clear liquid. A white label, boldly printed in red and bearing the skull and crossbones and the words "Deadly Poison," was pasted across the front.

"You damn Finnlander, whatcha trying to do? Poison me?" Jim bellowed.

The poor Finn's spirits fell to a low ebb. "No, no!" he remonstrated. "That good rink, that good moon," he replied.

Jim read the label. "It says here, deadly poison."

"No! That old bottle. I make. Me fill it," he explained.

Jim pulled the cork, smelled the contents, and then took a swallow, but the label had curbed his appetite. "Well, Charley," he said, "I'll let you go this time, but if I catch you trapping beaver again, you'll go to jail."

Relief spread all over the Finn's face as we moved on down the trail to his shack.

The place was immaculate, and we immediately accepted an invitation to dinner. "You like *mojakka*?" Charley inquired. Jim was familiar with the concoction, but it was my first experience with a Finnish stew. Fish is substituted for meat, and the ingredients are rather highly seasoned with salt, whole black pepper, and bay leaves. Mixed with whatever vegetables are available, the fish is allowed to cook until the meat falls away from the ribs and backbone. These are then lifted out and the meal is ready to serve. Charley's vegetables consisted of potatoes, carrots, and onions, and it was not a bad combination at all, although it did not sound very appetizing to me when I first learned of its contents. Jim was not partial to fish and suggested that we roast the beaver tail as a supplement to the meal. This sounded less palatable to me than the stew, but I found it very delicious and not unlike the tender buttery kernel of fat found in a T-bone steak. Had I been able to erase from my mind the ratty appearance of the tail before it was skinned, seasoned, and browned to a crisp, I am sure I would have enjoyed it immensely.

On the rafters in Charley's cabin were stored a dozen or more birch saplings about seven inches in diameter, each pair showing a progressively longer period of seasoning. They were carefully selected, with an almost identical natural bend in each that described about the same arc. This was ski timber from which, each year, Charley shaped a new pair of skis. The wood was not used until it had aged for at least seven years, during which time it thoroughly dried out and hardened, to prevent splitting. When his skis were placed on the snow, only the tip and rear touched, the center being fully six inches off the ground. When the weight of the skier was applied, the skis flattened out, thereby distributing the weight of the load pretty uniformly along their full length. This made for a flat surface on the snow and the greatest amount of support for the skier. After my enlightenment, it was no wonder to me that a good pair of traveling skis could not be had for under fifty dollars. Skis will increase a man's speed about a mile an hour over snowshoes, and I bought a pair of old ones from Charley on which to practice.

One of my first experiences, after learning to stand up on them and move along with some degree of alacrity on level ground, caused me to stick to snowshoes. Returning from town one afternoon with a small pack on my back, I was slipping along easily over the snow through the timber when I came to a sloping hillside. The only obstructions in my path were a few pine stumps, but there was a wide, clear path down the center, all the way to the bottom. I thought it would be fun to whiz down the incline and accordingly placed myself pointing straight ahead and down the passage and pushed off. The snow was just right, and I gained speed rapidly, the scenery rushing by on both sides of me, but not so with one stump. Try as I would, I kept veering off until it was directly in my path, and the climax was inevitable. One ski and my packsack continued on down the hill, but I brought up suddenly and with considerable force, lying over the top of the stump on my stomach, the wind knocked completely out of me. When I came to, I gathered up my belongings and limped painfully into camp, but from then on the skis served only as an ornamentation for my cabin wall.

Jim and I made a big two-day circle, staying overnight at a Canadian ranger's cabin on an island in Basswood Lake. There was no special effort to uncover evaders of the trapping laws; at that time it was generally conceded that anyone with the fortitude to wrest a living from the wilds was entitled to what he caught, provided he took out a license. Jim himself was not averse to another good meal of illegal moose meat before he took off for town.

It was time to make another missionary trip to headquarters in the interests of good fellowship. Bill was there in the old chair with his pipe. I knew there was something wrong the moment I opened the door. His face was an ugly, threatening black cloud. His eyes snapped angrily. Without a preliminary greeting, in a harsh, wrathful, possessive voice, he snapped out, "You caught my black beaver, didn't you?"

In a flash, I knew what he referred to. Apparently he had also stumbled onto the dam on the little creek before the pond froze over and had seen the black ones at work. I felt that this was the end; Bill would never forgive my finding his secret treasure. Innocently, I inquired, "What black beaver and how come yours?"

"You know damn well what ones. Them was on my territory," he retorted.

"If I recall correctly," I told him, "I offered to split the territory with you last fall in any manner or direction you chose and told you distinctly that if you refused I would consider it open to either of us. You refused, and I definitely remember telling you we would go it alone wherever we chose so long as that was your wish. You have no kick coming just because I uncovered one of your secrets."

He was close to an apoplectic stroke, he was so mad, but he said nothing more to me. I speeded up my preparations to leave immediately as I had no wish to spend the night with him in his ugly frame of mind.

It was late, and my best bet was the O'Niel shack. I could

make it by ten o'clock that night. There was a full moon as I set out, and it was cold and clear. A fox's "yip—yip—arooo" on a nearby hill sent a little tingle down my spine. It was good hunting weather. The trail led along a ridge of virgin mixed timber, huge hemlocks, pine, maple, birch, elm, ash, and basswood. A pack of wolves started a deer off in the distance and I heard their deep bass voices faintly as they bayed on the moonlit trail. It is a blood-curdling sound, but the old-time trappers claim there has never been a proven incident where wolves have attacked a human being. Even though I had heard them many times before, my pace quickened. The racket continued louder and louder, and as the deep baying notes became clearer and trembled on the motionless air of the silent night, I looked back from time to time, for I felt that they must be close behind me on the trail. I had no gun, and in spite of my many nights alone in the deep forest, I didn't like it.

At last I came in sight of the cabin, and felt better. On my arrival, I built a fire and went out to the root house for some provisions. The pack were still coming and their deep baying gave way to an occasional excited yip as one of the trailers momentarily caught sight of the prey. I closed the root house doors. There was now a chorus of excited yips. Yip, yip—yip—yip; on they came. I listened for a moment and was about to return to the shack when an enormous buck crashed into the clearing. He came between the root house and the shack, running silently, not twenty feet away. I could hear his labored breathing and see his steaming breath and frost-coated whiskers. His tongue hung out and dangled loosely from the side of his mouth. As he passed I caught a bluish reflection in his eyes that told me he was old and tired and that the end was not far off.

In less than a minute after he had passed, eleven large timber wolves came bounding through, intense and eager, hot on the trail, their large, bushy tails describing circles in the air as they loped easily along. They did not seem to be in any hurry, but their bright eyes flashed fire and excitement as they watched the trail ahead. Intermittently one would let out a sharp "yip, yip," but they were so intent on closing in on their quarry that they never saw my silent form leaning against the frame of the root house door. The chorus went on for probably another five minutes, rising in tempo as they gained on their prey. Then, with a final crescendo, all was silent. The buck had turned at bay. The chase was over, and there was nothing left for the pursuers to do now but cut down their prize and rip him to shreds with their strong white teeth. Another saga of the wilds was ended.

APRIL WAS ALREADY HERE. I covered more ground in the next week than I ever had before. Weasel were so badly stained canary yellow that their once-white pelts were practically worthless, and I caught more and more mink that showed slight signs of rubbing. One day I came across fresh beaver cuttings. The family had apparently run out of food and, each taking his turn, they had placed their warm backs against the undersurface of the lake ice and laboriously melted a hole through to freedom and fresh bark. This lake had a rocky shoreline, and they were forced to their unusual tactics by the fact that they did not have any runways into marshy areas where tender grass shoots and nodules are usually available to piece out their dwindling food supplies.

I expected Oscar Johnson any day now and got things in shape to concentrate on the "pigs," the name by which beaver are known to all trappers, for the short month prior to the spring breakup. I pulled everything but my beaver sets and placed all usable traps near new dams and beaver houses discovered during the winter. There were dozens of new bows ready to receive the hides. The new traps were provided with long heavy fish cord leads to allow the animals to head for deep water when they are startled by the snap of the trap's jaws on their legs. All of my pelts were on their boards or bundled for transporting to town, and I was ready for the severe test of strength and endurance that always accompanies the spring rush of beaver trapping. In three short weeks after breakup you work against time, cover endless miles of territory, visit hundreds of dams and beaver houses, and take as many pelts as you have the energy to handle in your waking hours.

Oscar came in that night with a hundred and twenty-five traps. We now had three hundred and fifty number one-and-a-half double-spring units between us. He couldn't take his eyes off the many hides I had already taken and was anxious to get started at once. I drew out a map of the countryside, located all of the lakes and streams for him, and marked the dams and beaver houses in their proper places. Where there was running water, the ice had already melted along the dams and around the houses, and the lakes showed signs that the ice was beginning to shift, so that there would soon be strips of open water along the windward shores. These were ideal conditions. The beaver were hungry and there were plenty of open places for underwater sets. I was hungry, too, and we dined sumptuously that night on two-inch steaks that Oscar brought from town; he knew my weakness when it came to meat.

Oscar was an experienced trapper, but I accompanied him for the first day in our mutual interests and we exchanged a few kinks and wrinkles that improved both our techniques. He went on ahead to prove out the authenticity of my map, and his ability to follow it, and that day we set and baited all of the traps he had brought in with him. It now remained to set the traps I had made ready and cached earlier in the week.

In addition to a long cord on the trap chain, beaver traps must have a large flat stone wired to their undersides for weight. When a beaver is caught, instinct warns him to escape through the water, which is his natural medium. The stone must be small enough for him to be able to drag the weight to the full length of the chain cord, but heavy enough so that after his struggles to free himself, he does not have wind or strength to lift the weight and come to the surface for air. If they get back to dry land, they immediately chew off their leg and escape, and all you have is a leathery, long clawed foot to show for your trouble. As painful as it must be, the loss of a foot is not fatal, and I have caught many a beaver where the fur had completely overgrown the stub of a leg that had been amputated in a previous encounter with a steel trap.

We went to work in earnest. Oscar took one line and I

took the other. At the end of the week, we changed to provide new scenery for both of us, and to offer new ideas to tempt the wary ones that had escaped our earlier efforts. At night we skinned, sewed, and stretched the hides onto the bows until our sleepy eyes closed while our fingers were still working. I don't believe we averaged over four-and-a-half hours' sleep a night, but the golden harvest pyramided higher and higher.

We worked the creeks and ponds, always being careful to leave enough for seed in each location to restock the area for another season. Beaver are very prolific and produce anywhere from two to fourteen young a year. Oscar's one obsession was to bring a more valuable catch than I did: larger hides, greater number, or more blacks. It made no difference, as long as the money value was there. I believe in the end I had caught seventeen more than he had, with about a proportionate increase in dollar value, which rankled him slightly, but we got on famously and I enjoyed the companionship of our evenings together immensely.

The lakes took on a dirty, sullen scowl. For two or three weeks, the ice would be unsafe and we would be practically cut off from town and sources of supply. Oscar and I had taken stock of our provisions and decided we had enough to go through the breakup. We had close to twenty-five pounds of flour, ten pounds of sugar, half a slab of bacon, a pound of salt, some oatmeal, and a few minor items, including four fifteen-cent cans of tobacco that Oscar chewed and smoked alternately, and I had one carton of cigarettes.

One day I came in early. It was about two o'clock. Some visitors had brought us a huge fillet of fresh-caught landlocked salmon. The fish lay across our kitchen table and hung over on each end a good six inches. The meat was a beautiful delicate pink and must have weighed easily thirty pounds. That would mean a fish of no less than seventy pounds in the round, head and all. Hanging down from the table in front of the fish, one end caught underneath the meat, were four sheets of toilet paper from our roll on the shelf. In very faint pencil scrawls, there was a note that read: "Dear boys. We got no grub so we tuk wat we kud fine. Will pay youse back in town. Sined Gunder Tekela. Waino Maki." This was an unexpected, crushing blow. Our entire supply of food was gone. The two Finnish boys were camped ten miles to the north of us on Cacaquabie [Kekekabic] Lake. They had run out of supplies and were cut off from town, too. I had no other choice than to go after our food before they ate it up. We knew the boys well and were sure they had no intention of taking all our food. They just didn't realize that we were almost in the same predicament they were in, but I felt that under the circumstances, it was up to them to make the long, tedious hundred-mile overland trip to town and not us.

I took a straight compass course for their cabin and got into almost as much trouble as the trip to town would have been. Three miles from the lake, I ran into a thick tamarack blowdown. The smooth, weathered, barkless spikes were piled up like jackstraws in all directions. I was up and over, then down and under, to the right, to the left, and then backward to extricate myself from the sharp, spearlike branches that caught at and tore my clothes in a dozen places. I traveled twice the distance that would have been necessary without the obstructions.

Shortly after I entered the morass, I came upon a nice fat moose lying under the thicket of impenetrable trees and branches. He had been paunched by a high-power bullet and had worked his way into this tangle to evade his pursuers and die. The body was well preserved and still half covered with snow. He had likely been killed in the fall, and I don't doubt but that the meat would have still been edible. He had certainly been under refrigeration for the entire winter.

Finally, I worked my way through to their camp and found most of our groceries, still intact. The boys were not in, and it was my turn to leave a note. I didn't have the heart to take back everything, but figured out starvation rations for ourselves, left the meager balance for them, and returned to camp, this time by the trail.

When I arrived, it was eleven o'clock, and Oscar had worn a groove in the floor pacing from his chair to the door. Neither of us had been out that late before since we had been together except by prearranged agreement. I have thought a hundred times since of the critical position I would have been in had I broken a leg in jumping from one tree trunk to another in my wet slippery packs. No one knew where I was, I had destroyed the note from our neighbors, and the fish and absence of our supplies was a complete mystery to my partner until I had time to relate the tale on my return.

The lake ice pulled away from the shore and we changed our locations. When the wind was right, we could make many of our runs by canoe and our harvest jumped back up again, even with the ice moving in and pushing our sets up on shore night after night, completely ruining many a night's catch. The lake beaver were hungrier and started foraging before the sun went down. We took as high as three beaver out of a single trap in one night. Oscar and I were nothing but skin, bones, and sinew, but we loved it!

At last the breakup came. The wind whipped around into the west and sent down powerful blasts of warm chinook breezes. Overnight, the lake ice broke up into spear-sharp tinkling splinters of honeycomb that built up into beautiful crystal palaces along the shore, pushed there by the inexorable weight of huge cakes of floe ice that drifted down the lake with the high winds.

We waited for the lake to clear and, for diversion, decided to see how Charley the Finn was making it. When we got to his cabin, it was empty. I could smell woodsmoke strongly and there was another peculiar odor mingled with it, reminiscent of the bottle Charley had offered Jim on the previous visit I had made him. Oscar and I followed our noses about a hundred yards down the hill into a swamp. Presently we could see wisps of blue smoke drifting toward us through the spruce and cedar. The next moment, we were looking down the barrel of a thirty-thirty caliber rifle. Charley recognized us almost immediately and put down the gun. "Maybe you pretty near get shot," he said, grinning sheepishly. "I make a little moon," he whispered, proud of his secret. "You like a little rink?" he offered hospitably. We didn't say no, and he beckoned us to follow him.

In the next thickets, we almost ran into a hut before Oscar and I noticed it. Built of poles, set upright in the ground, thatched with pine boughs, it blended into the protective covering of the surrounding foliage so well we would have missed it had we been alone. Charley disappeared behind a bushy spruce that covered the door and shortly came out with a jug. The contents had just been drawn off and the "moon" was lukewarm. A taste was enough for me. I barely wet my lips. How anyone could drink the vile stuff—and I am not a teetotaler—I cannot tell you. We praised his concoction, however, and were invited to inspect his still.

I have never seen a queerer contrivance, yet it showed considerable ingenuity, too. In the center of the one-room hut stood a stone fireplace connected at the back by three lengths of stovepipe to a hole in the roof. A copper wash boiler sat on the stones, its heavily sooted bottom resting over the fire pit. The convex cover had been inverted so that it hung down into the body of the boiler, where it was held snugly in place by the reversed band that had been soldered to the outer edge. The cover handle had been replaced by a strap iron rack constructed to hold a small enameled pan just above the boiling contents of the still and directly beneath the apex of the inverted cover. Charley fermented his corn-meal mush in a large oak cask in the corner of the room and drew off the findings through a wooden spigot placed near the bottom. These he put in the boiler to cook. The cover was filled with snow, which caused the steam from the boiling liquid to condense on its underside and run down into the enamel collecting pan on the rack. When the pan filled, Charley emptied it into the jug and it was ready for use. That was all there was to it. We had a good laugh on the way back to our shack. That was an easier business than trapping.

We could go almost anyplace now by canoe, and we worked in our shirtsleeves in the warm spring air. Our route was short enough so that we could make faster time traveling together in one canoe, covering fully as much territory as would have been possible had we gone our separate ways. One held the canoe in position while the other picked up the fur and reset the traps.

There was a big dam on one of the upper lakes that had been exceptionally fruitful. We had several sets in that area and went up to pull our traps and pick up any remaining fur they had picked up in our absence. We approached a set Oscar had made on the dam itself. He was in the bow, and I nosed him in close, so that he could make his pickup. The trap was gone. We had moved along four or five feet of the dam, Oscar holding the prow in close with his paddle, when a large animal just over the line of the dam hurled its body at the canoe. Oscar was so startled he fell over backwards into the bottom. A large beaver, one hind leg held firmly in the trap, had cut a deep gouge in the canvas of our bow. I laughed heartily and nosed him in again. Oscar backed away, but after kidding him a while I put him ashore on the dam, where he found a stout cudgel and put an end to his captive. It was one of the largest we had caught and Oscar had him by his only remaining leg. The other three had been cut off and the stumps were completely grown over, making a solid ball of fur except for the one that held him in our trap.

The females were almost all heavy with young, and the males we caught had holes in their hides where the expectant mothers had chased and bitten them to clear the house for the changeover to its use as a nursery. One old fellow who had apparently refused to vacate had sixty holes in his useless hide when he finally stumbled into our trap.

It was time to stop. We gathered in our sets and took a

breathing spell of two days; we got out of bed only long enough to eat our meals and enjoyed a well-earned rest.

During the last week of heavy trapping, we ran out of bows and stretched and tacked some forty beaver pelts to the barkless trunks of some hemlock stubs, no doubt remnants left by the same storm that laid low the forest on Expectancy. We assumed the pelts to be dry enough to pick up and paddled over to get them. It was not far from where I had found the bear denned up for the winter, and I told Oscar about my foolish urge to pike the old fellow as I went by on the trail. I showed him the spot, and you could still see the impression in the bed of leaves where his great body had lain in peaceful hibernation, but he had long been gone.

When we arrived at the hemlocks our hides were gone, too—every last one of them. We were at the right spot all right, for the tacks were still there, and little tufts of fur clung to some of them. We found long claw marks on the tree trunks that told us our thief was unquestionably a bear. I examined the ground and found sets of claw marks there, too. Noting the direction they pointed in, I followed carefully, and in thirty feet picked up a small kit that had evidently slipped from the animal's grasp. The tracks seemed awfully fresh, but it was necessary to proceed slowly in order to stay on the trail. Twenty-five yards further on, I picked up four more hides. Eventually we recovered every last one of them. Nine were badly mutilated and torn, but we were glad they were not a total loss. I advanced the theory that they had been taken just prior to our arrival and because of their slippery nature had been dropped a few at a time until our scent caused the plunderer to abandon the balance and leave abruptly. A beaver hide is very greasy, and I have no doubt they were carried away for some hungry cubs who never got the chance to lick off the grease.

Coming in a few days later from one of our explorations of the countryside, we followed a trail along the shore of the lake to the east of our camp at the narrows. Below the dam, in the short stretch of rapid river connecting the two lakes, we discovered thousands upon thousands of spawning tullibees or whitefish. They were packed into the stream so tight that the top fish were pushed half out of the water, and there was a constant struggle among them to get down underneath before they suffocated, which kept the mass of flashing silver in continuous motion. The river itself was forced out of its bed by these finny obstructions, the water overflowing its banks and running off between the marshy hummocks on both sides. Had they been stationary and of a less slippery nature, it would have been an easy matter to cross the stream on their backs without wetting a foot, where normally the water was two feet deep. Just back of this struggling hoard, in the deeper water of the narrows, we discovered several hundred enormous northern pike, fat, lazy fellows, many of them longer than a canoe paddle, that we estimated to weigh well over thirty pounds. They lay there suspended inanimately in about four feet of water. All they had to do to obtain their food was to move ahead a few feet and chop with their sawlike teeth a few of the stragglers in the school of tullibees, much as you would bite off a tender crust of pie. Seating ourselves, we watched this phenomenon of reproduction and nature's version of the law of supply and demand with great interest and in rapt silence.

In the sunlit warmth of the beautiful days that followed, we took our guns and scoured the hillsides for big game that would be a welcome change for the Johnson family in town. Most of the animals either had or were giving birth to their offspring and held close to their well-chosen hideouts during this period. We saw surprisingly few animals of any kind.

We were in no particular hurry to leave but had about given up hopes of providing for the Johnsons when, as Oscar and I topped a ridge we were crossing, about fifty yards apart, I came face to face with a large female black bear and her two cubs coming from the opposite side. She wasn't twenty feet away, and she was just as startled as I was. Slowly she rose on her hind legs and bared her glistening, curved white teeth in a low snarling growl. My presence of mind returned in this emergency and I leveled my rifle at her head. I couldn't miss at that range. Oscar, I learned later, had seen the whole performance and had gone into action, also. Simultaneously our rifles cracked, and the mother went down in a heap. I had sent a bullet into her brain. The cubs didn't know what to do, and I easily dropped them one at a time with a neck shot that saved all the meat. Oscar came over and laughingly showed me a neat hole in the mother's side, just over her heart. "I thought you would never snap out of it, so I put in this one just in case," he informed me. I had never heard his shot at all. The cubs were good-sized for early June, and would no doubt make delicious eating. It took two trips to bring in the meat, and we were now committed to a trip to town within the next few days as it was warming up even in the deepest swamps, where there was a little snow left, and we would not be able to hold the meat for long.

We got out the folding canoe and gave the canvas a new coat of waterproofing. It proved as tight as a hot water bottle, and was ready for service. We bundled our furs, stacked our stretching boards to save the next occupant of the cabin endless hours of work, made a flying trip to the O'Niel shack and picked up the odds and ends we had left there, swept it out and left it in as good shape as we had found it, and were ready to leave in the morning. We had been working against time for three days and were practically out of everything. Oscar was smoking his recovered dried-out tobacco quids in his pipe, and I was scavenging the cabin and landscape for cigarette butts that I emptied out of the paper and smoked in mine. We were desperate—out of tobacco, flour, sugar, salt, and about everything else but fish, meat, and oatmeal. If you have ever tried any of these three items without seasoning of any kind, you can understand our predicament.

All beaver required a three-dollar state tag to make them legal, but there was little reason to expect to run into a game warden in this lonely section, so we decided to turn renegades and run them in, taking our chances. Each spring, a group of at least a dozen wardens gather at the upper end of the border lakes and come down the chain en masse, picking up those unfortunate trappers who happen to have also chosen that fateful day for their exodus. The rest usually come through without difficulty. I hesitate to say what the result would be of a chance meeting in the wilderness of a lone game warden and a determined trapper with three thousand dollars' worth of fur that represented his entire year's earnings and endless hours of lonely toil. I can only say that were I the warden, I would want the drop on the culprit and would take great pains to make sure he did not see me first.

We came down our little-used chain of lakes in daylight and planned to hit the border after dark. Halfway down to the headquarters shack, my heart stood still. A canoe with two figures in it approached. We didn't know whether to run for it or bluff it through. If they were wardens, they would soon overtake our two heavily laden canoes. If we took to the woods, all we could save would be our guns and the two most valuable packs. We decided to go through and were greatly relieved to make out Bill and another young fellow from town as we shortened the distance between us. Bill surveyed our bulging packs with envious eyes as we passed, but the only greeting he offered was "Hi." We stopped at headquarters and picked up my bundles of pelts that I had ready there. You could barely see over the tops of the loads in either canoe from the seats in the stern.

The first border portage into Basswood was the most dangerous, and I fully expected disaster to overtake us here, where I had experienced so many misfortunes on previous trips. It was nine o'clock as we concealed our canoes in the bushes and started bringing our loads across. At midnight, nothing had happened; we were over the portage and off again for a four-mile paddle down the lake. We kept to the shadows and made another, little-used portage, avoiding the Indian village and Four-mile Portage for obvious reasons, although it cost us three extra short portages on the way down. We traveled by night and slept what little we could in the daytime, concealing our canoes in unlikely marshy bays and inlets. It was our plan to cover the last lake into town so that we would unload at the Johnson home just before daylight in the morning. I was a little afraid to attempt it at the town house because of Bill's ill feeling and the fact that everyone knew I had trapped all winter.

Our arrival was according to timetable, and we docked at the pump house where the mill had formerly taken its water from the lake for the boilers. It was two-thirty. The village was as quiet as a cemetery, and at four we were unloaded and had paddled our canoes around the main dock and turned them upside down on the planking. We both gave a deep sigh of relief, had a large lunch, and went to bed.

I stayed at Johnson's for the balance of the night, but slept very little. To my surprise, there seemed to be other visitors sharing my bed, and to be sure, when I got up, I had several red welts on my body that itched like fury. We had a good breakfast of ham and eggs that put me back to normal and ended our fast.

After breakfast, Mr. Smith came over and appraised our fur. My personal pelts came to eight hundred dollars; our joint catch figured another eighteen hundred. We made a deal and agreed to deliver them at the Smith residence. It was only half a block away, and with the help of two of his brothers, Oscar and I boldly transferred one pack at a time in broad daylight without encountering a soul. Mr. Smith made out a nine-hundred-dollar check to Oscar and one for seventeen hundred dollars to me. We were both highly pleased with our success.

The next week, Mrs. Smith made a mysterious visit to Chicago, a large fur-buying center where there are no game laws covering beaver. As she boarded the train, you would conclude that she was taking an extended European tour from the size of the four large trunks on which she paid excess at the baggage depot.

I was undergoing an intense mental turmoil. In the wilderness, my overhead did not exceed over five hundred dollars a year, including as many pleasure trips to the village and county seat as I had any desire for. In a very short time, I could lay away, in sound securities, enough to keep me for the rest of my life. It was a clean, peaceful, healthful existence. I was in an environment that was entirely to my liking, and I derived an untold amount of pleasure out of observing the wild creatures in their natural haunts. In fact, I was producing all the arguments I could possibly dream up to sell myself the idea of forsaking the outer world and permanently turning sourdough. On the other hand, my conscience kept whispering in my ear that my forefathers had all been businessmen—that it was my duty to my folks and myself to make more of my life than just being a trapper. In the end, my conscience won and I sorrowfully set about my preparations to leave.

The first thing was to sell off my traps, then my camping equipment, and finally my guns, with the exception of my two favorites, a shotgun and a rifle. I could not bear to part with them, nor to so positively sever the last tie that bound me to a possible future trip to some hunting grounds somewhere as a short respite from the marital and business cares that were definite prospects in my future.

I filled the tires of the flivver with air, took it off the blocks, bought a new battery, and coaxed the car over to the gas station, where it was washed, greased, and serviced. The backseat was practically empty, my suitcase, two guns, a dunnage bag full of souvenirs, and six hundred fine prime rats for a Hudson seal coat for my mother being all I had left. Nearly all my friends were there to see me off. Even Bill* showed up and shook hands in a friendly good-bye. I kicked the starter, and with a final wave was off down the road. The exhaust sang a little tune: "Put, put, put, put, put it all behind you." I had never known a deeper grief. Slowly I was aware the tune had changed: "But, but, but, but you'll be back," it added with firm determination.

THAT WAS THIRTY-THREE YEARS AGO. I am standing now on the site of our headquarters shack, or rather nearly so, for I am crowded off to one side by a spacious summer home. I have just completed the rounds of my old haunts to the extent that my young guide deemed advisable. In reality, he is not a guide, for I could follow the waterways and portages with my eyes shut, but he has a strong back that carries my dunnage over the portages and muscular arms that paddle my canoe swiftly and silently over the blue waters of the lakes. The islands and wooded points are dotted with cabins, and the shores are lined with little docks and swimming floats. Power launches and white sails dot the bay and raucous speedboats blast their way in criss-

---

* By about 1925, Bill Berglund operated a small hunting and fishing resort on the east end of Knife Lake, where he was later joined by Dorothy Molter, the Root Beer Lady. Berglund died in 1948.

cross patterns, crashing the silence that used to be. A huge seaplane, motors idling, glides, whistling in for a landing, the cabin crowded with commuters from the city.

My mind went back to Jim O'Niel, who, like me, returned for a last look at the wilderness he loved so well, and then wished to stay and die in the cabin where he had spent so many happy hours. I could appreciate his sentiment, but I did not want to stay. It was not the same. The romance was dead. The wilderness had been desecrated by advancing civilization, its chastity invaded by the human hordes. Had I realized the change that had taken place, I would rather have stayed away, living in my dream world of fond memories, than to have witnessed this sacrilege, this profanation of a hushed and silent forest inhabited only by the wild creatures that now had left to make room for the advancing throngs. I turned my back on the scene, an old man, left behind by the changing times.

PUBLISHER'S AFTERWORD

CHARLES IRA COOK JR. embarked on his 1919–20 adventure at a time of transition in northeastern Minnesota's Boundary Waters. Today's readers will find his descriptions of its colorful inhabitants, wild terrain, and abundant animal life evocative of a long-ago era, but they may also note the signs of development that appear on his horizon almost daily.

Traveling and trapping in northern Lake and St. Louis Counties, Cook repeatedly encountered remnants of the area's short-lived mining and lumbering booms—abandoned camps, dams, sluices, portages, roads. In 1882 gold, silver, and iron-ore strikes had aroused intense commercial interest in the Quetico-Superior country. Iron ore was in fact responsible for the platting of the village of Ely five years later and for construction of the Iron Range Railway that linked it to Duluth in 1888.

At about the same time, timber companies that had recently depleted Michigan's pine lands turned hungrily to northeastern Minnesota's forests. Acquiring white pine stands in great tracts, they began substantial logging near Ely in 1892 when G. W. Knox Lumber Company built a large sawmill on Fall Lake and founded the village of Winton. A half-dozen years later, the Swallow and Hopkins Lumber Company constructed a logging railroad along the four-mile Basswood portage frequently traversed by Cook; railroad flatcars helped carry logs out from the network of waterways created by low log dams. By the late 1910s, logging in the area was drawing to a close, and, as Cook observed, the uninterrupted virgin forests of red and white pine and white spruce were gone—except across the Canadian border. Replacing them were sometimes fire-blackened stands of scrub jackpine, spruce, balsam, poplar, and popple (aspen).

Cook's trapping sojourn coincided with changes in the human history, as well as the natural history, of Minnesota's Boundary Waters. Some seven million acres of Ojibwe lands in what is now northeastern Minnesota had been taken by the Treaty of La Pointe in 1854, and a related treaty with the Bois Forte band a dozen years later created Minnesota's Nett Lake reservation just forty miles south of Canada and west of the border lakes. Not all native people moved to or stayed on reservation lands, however. Some returned to favored forest clearings and waterways, where they joined others who also preferred to live and work there. Families such as Leo Chosa's and Joe Pete's maintained high enough profiles to be counted by 1920 census enumerators who ventured into Lake and St. Louis Counties; more elusive individuals did not. In contrast to the area's many Finnish, Scandinavian, and Slovenian immigrants, these families were among the very few who listed their place of birth as the United States—usually Minnesota, Wisconsin, or Michigan. Along with a sprinkling of rogues and loners such as Bill Berglund, people in the Boundary Waters community hunted, trapped, and fished as necessary or as permitted by treaty with the United States government, rather than as proscribed by state game laws. They also imbibed home brew or smuggled Canadian liquor, sometimes sharing their illegal caches with tolerant game wardens.

Increasingly, these local residents found themselves

interacting with outsiders like Cook who eagerly explored the region. A dozen years earlier, in response to aggressive lobbying by Minnesotans seeking to preserve the border lakes, President Theodore Roosevelt had established the one-million-acre Superior National Forest. Local newspaper accounts of canoe routes and publication in 1916 of the first Boundary Waters canoe map by the Duluth and Iron Range Railway accelerated the curiosity of outsiders. The rapid development of roads into the region and construction of primitive fishing camps on Clearwater and Burntside Lakes exposed other hardy visitors to the area's charms before World War I curtailed these pleasure excursions.

Postwar promotion of auto tourism in the Ely, Duluth, Minneapolis, and St. Paul newspapers, however, resulted in the first small flood of visitors to places like Winton. Outfitters including Leo Chosa could be hired to show tenderfeet where to fish, hunt, and portage. By 1922 Minnesota's northeastern forest had become accessible by automobile at three points: Crane Lake, Ely, and Grand Marais.

Not everyone approved. During the 1920s, conservation groups defeated a series of ambitious proposals to build roads through the area and to dam chains of lakes and rivers for hydroelectric power. In 1930 Congress passed the Shipstead-Newton-Nolan act protecting the shorelines of lakes and streams, and the state followed in 1933 with a similar law. Coincidentally, the Great Depression reduced the number of visitors seeking guides and accommodations, forcing some residents to move elsewhere.

In the 1940s, over objections from resort owners worried about loss of livelihood, new laws forbade access by seaplane and roads to the interior lakes. By the time the aging Cook revisited his haunts around 1950, the process of buying up remaining resorts and summer homes for conversion to wilderness had already begun.

Additions to the protected region since that time make today's Boundary Waters Canoe Area Wilderness more than one million acres in size. Part of the almost four-million-acre Superior National Forest, the BWCA stretches one hundred fifty miles along the Canadian border, contains more than a thousand lakes larger than ten acres, has twelve hundred miles of canoe routes, and is visited by more than two hundred thousand people a year. Cook would surely sigh—but perhaps not be surprised—to learn that eighty years after his first visit, the Boundary Waters has become the most heavily used wilderness area in the country.

SOURCES

The most thorough history of the Boundary Waters Canoe Area Wilderness is found in R. Newell Searle's *Saving Quetico-Superior: A Land Set Apart* (Minnesota Historical Society Press, 1977). Also full of details is J. Wesley White's bound volume of mimeographed articles, "Historical Sketches of the Quetico-Superior" (1967–69), prepared for the U.S. Forest Service; a copy is available at the Minnesota Historical Society Library, St. Paul.

Aviator Charles Ira Cook Jr.

Cook (second from right), with fellow air-service officers

Cook with his small canoe

A young "loon" in the canoe

Bill Berglund at border marker near Saganaga Lake

Berglund with packs

A campsite with Berglund crouching in the shadows near a bough-covered tent and pelts drying on stretchers

Rocky cliffs at Cypress Lake

The village of North Lake, Ontario

An unidentified falls in the Boundary Waters

Canadian rangers

Catch of fish, mostly northern pike and probably used for dogfood

The Joe Pete family, including infants in cradleboards, at Basswood Lake

Jenny Pete (Boshey) and Mary Pete (O'Leary),
daughters of Joe and Marie Pete

Marie and Joe Pete
and other family members

A drowned beaver caught in a trap

The building that probably served as Cook's base in Winton

A large beaver pelt on alder-bow stretcher, displayed with hunting rifle, ax, traps, and other drying pelts

*Cook preparing
a camp meal*

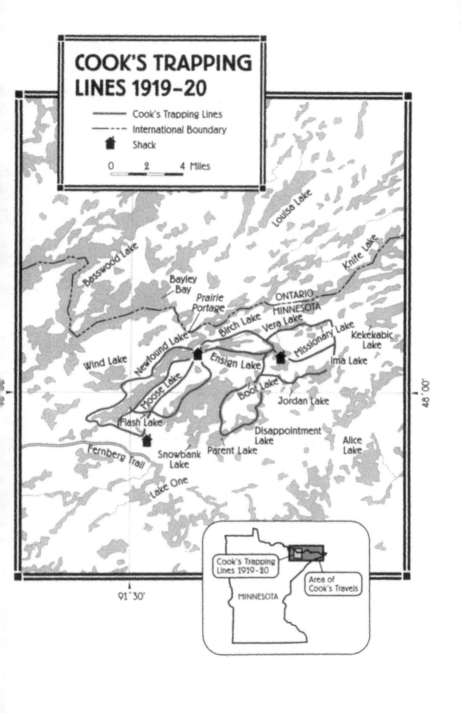

COOK'S TRAPPING LINES 1919–20

—————— Cook's Trapping Lines
- - - - - - International Boundary
🏠 Shack

0   2   4 Miles

Louisa Lake

Knife Lake

Basswood Lake

Bayley Bay

Prairie Portage

ONTARIO
MINNESOTA

Birch Lake

Vera Lake

Missionary Lake

Kekekabic Lake

Wind Lake

Newfound Lake

Ensign Lake

Ima Lake

Moose Lake

Boot Lake

Jordan Lake

Flash Lake

Disappointment Lake

Alice Lake

Fernberg Trail

Snowbank Lake

Parent Lake

Lake One

48°00'

91°30'

Cook's Trapping Lines 1919–20

Area of Cook's Travels

MINNESOTA

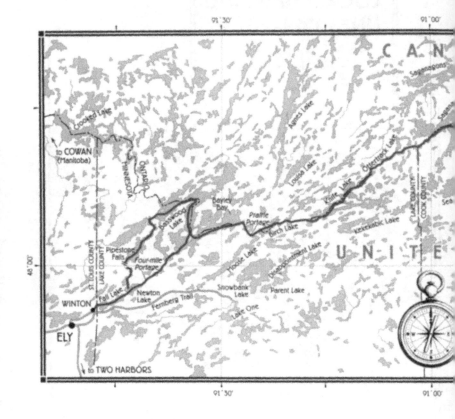

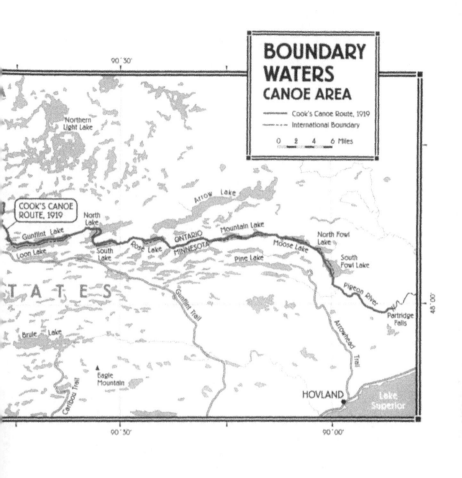

BOUNDARY WATERS CANOE AREA

――――― Cook's Canoe Route, 1919
‒ ‒ ‒ ‒ International Boundary

0   2   4   6 Miles

90°30'

Northern
Light Lake

Arrow Lake

COOK'S CANOE
ROUTE, 1919

North
Lake

Mountain Lake

Gunflint Lake

ONTARIO
MINNESOTA

Rose Lake

Moose Lake

North Fowl
Lake

Loon Lake

South
Lake

Pine Lake

South
Fowl Lake

T A T E S

Gunflint Trail

Pigeon River

46°00'

Partridge
Falls

Brule Lake

Eagle
Mountain

Arrowhead Trail

Caribou Trail

HOVLAND

Lake
Superior

90°30'

90°00'

Trapping the Boundary Waters
Designed and set in type by Will Powers
at the Minnesota Historical Society Press.
The text type is Figural, designed by
Oldrich Menhart in 1940.
The book was printed and bound
by Thomson-Shore, Inc., Dexter, Michigan.

Digital imaging of cover and interior photographs
by Lois Stanfield, LightSource Images.

Maps and text illustrations by Matt Kania.

Printed in the USA
CPSIA information can be obtained
at www.ICGtesting.com
JSHW082205140824
68134JS00014B/431